The Good Shepherd and His Little Lambs
Study Edition

The Good Shepherd and His Little Lambs Study Edition: A First Communion Story-Primer

Story by Mrs. Hermann Bosch

Supplement by Janet P. McKenzie

A RACE for Heaven Product

Biblio Resource Publications
108½ South Moore Street
Bessemer, MI 49911
2010

ISBN 978-1-934185-36-0

Published by Biblio Resource Publications, Inc.
108½ South Moore Street, Bessemer, MI 49911
info@biblioresource.com

A **R**ead **A**loud **C**urriculum **E**nrichment Product
www.RACEforHeaven.com

The following apply to the 1912 text only:
Nihil Obstat: Remigius Lafort, DD, *Censor*
Imprimatur: John Cardinal Farley, *Archbishop of New York*
New York
April 11, 1912

Printed in the United States of America

With much love,
this edition is dedicated to my grandchildren,
Althea, Grace, Norah, Ethan, and Katherine,
and all the other little lambs to come
with prayers that you may never stray
from the protective love of
our Good Shepherd.

Preface

The aim of this little book—to turn young souls to our Lord in the Blessed Sacrament—appeals to me so powerfully, that I deem it a privilege to commend it most warmly to the public, particularly to those seeking a suitable gift for First Communicants.

Knowing that little learners are not able to derive knowledge from lengthy deductions following abstract premises, Mrs. Bosch has formed a living picture of every notion she wishes to impart. The language placed upon the lips of the four youthful characters (Philip, Rose, John, and Anna) is adapted to the understanding of the very youngest.

After reading or hearing *The Good Shepherd and His Little Lambs*, the little ones will surely and clearly understand the real life and love of our dear Lord in the Blessed Sacrament.

A. Letellier, SSS
March 29, 1912
New York City, New York

Introduction

On August 8, 1910, Pope Pius X signed the Decree on First Communion (*Quam Singulari*), which lowered the age of first reception from twelve to seven years of age. This document followed his 1905 publication of *Sacred Tridentina* (Decree on Frequent and Daily Reception of Holy Communion). These two documents greatly contributed to not only more people receiving the Eucharist but also more frequently. Little wonder that Pope Pius X is often referred to as the "Pope of the Eucharist!"

It was perhaps in response to this lowering of the age for First Holy Communion that, in 1912, Mrs. Hermann Bosch wrote this engaging story to help young children prepare to receive our Lord in the Blessed Sacrament. More than a story, *The Good Shepherd and His Little Lambs* is a First Communion primer that takes the basic tenets of the catechism and, through naturally-flowing conversations, relates them in the language of little ones to authentic Christian living. Mrs. Bosch believed that preparation for First Holy Communion should consist in an understanding not only of the catechism but also of Jesus' great love for us. She explains, "We might learn the catechism all the way through beautifully, and at the end find ourselves still very stiff and clumsy about loving our Lord. When He comes to us, we don't want to welcome Him into our souls only with answers out of the catechism, do we?"

It is in this spirit that the 2010 edition of this delightful book has been prepared. While the text ensures that little ones will better know and serve our Lord Jesus, the supplemental material provides a gentle review of pertinent basic doctrine, connections to Scripture, prayers to memorize, poems to read aloud, and additional prayers to enrich a little lamb's spiritual life. Remember, however, that the supplemental material is provided to enrich the text—not to take center stage. Depending on each child's previous level of preparation, knowledge base, and intensity of interest, you may opt to use all, some, or none of the supplemental material. Please attach no guilt to any of these choices.

This book is best used as a read aloud—an experience shared with adults and children. Its easy narration of the simple truths of the Catholic faith and God's great love for us help to instill an endearing (and enduring) love of our Lord under the title of the Good Shepherd. It is my fervent prayer that this book will prompt many spiritual conversations and inspire you and your children to love our Lord in the Blessed Sacrament ever more deeply.

Janet P. McKenzie
March 19, 2010
Feast of St. Joseph

Table of Contents

"Feed My Lambs!"

THEY decided to have their talks in the back yard under the old elm trees—Auntie, who was big and knew a great many stories, and the four children, Rose and Anna, Philip and John.

Philip was nearly eight, and ever so much taller than his sister Rose and his cousin John, who were both seven. Anna was only six, and as she was as curly-headed and rosy-cheeked as a new doll, people would call her "the baby," no matter how many times she reminded them that her name was Anna.

"You needn't mind," said Auntie, picking Anna up and settling her upon her knee. "You're nearly as tall as your brother John, anyway."

"And John's seven," said Anna, very much soothed.

"Besides," said John, who was very fond and proud of his small sister, "I'm a boy, and boys have to be bigger than girls."

Auntie smiled at the manly little chap, who never willfully hurt anything—people, or their feelings, or birds or cats.

"If Anna gets too comfortable, Auntie," said Rose, watching Anna settling her head upon Auntie's shoulder, "she falls asleep."

"I don't!" cried Anna, sitting up straight.

"Well, if she does, no harm is done. She's our littlest lamb of all."

"But I'm not a baby," Anna declared, dropping back into cozy comfort. "I don't mind being a little lamb."

"No, not a baby," Auntie agreed. "And the little lambs are exactly what we want to talk about this morning. See, there are some on the hill over there. Aren't they pretty?"

A large flock of sheep moved lazily about upon the hill Auntie pointed out, and among them soft, little, white lambs frisked and played as all little lambs do on warm, sunny days.

"They're so pretty," said Rose. "One belongs to me. Father said so. And I put a blue ribbon around its neck, Auntie, and it knows me."

"Of course it knows you. Like Jesus said He knew His sheep, and they know Him. He called Himself the Good Shepherd, our Good Shepherd, and it seems to me that, while we are getting ready for First Communion, there is no sweeter name we can give Him."

All the children smiled. First Communion! This was May, and in two months more they were—all except Anna—to receive First Communion in the village church.

"And we're the Good Shepherd's little lambs," said John.

"His very little ones," said Auntie. "The littler we are, the more care and attention He must give us, you know."

"Like," said John gently, "we big children sit on the wooden seat, but Anna, because she's the baby, has the best place on Auntie's lap."

"I'm glad I'm the littlest," said Anna, for once not vexed at being the baby, "because it's very comfy here," burying her curly head more deeply into Auntie's shoulder. "I've a lovely picture about Jesus," she went on, "with all the sheep around Him, and some lambs, too, close up to His feet; but, Auntie, do you know what?"

Auntie looked down into the eager shining eyes.

"No, darling. What?"

"The very littlest lamb of all is on Jesus' shoulders—being carried!" Anna gazed in triumph over the group of children. How did they feel about being the baby now? "The reason," Anna finished with dignity, "that Jesus carried the poor, tired little lamb was just because it was the baby."

Rose and Philip smiled, but John said heartily, "Of course."

"The Good Shepherd will carry us, too," said Auntie, "when we grow tired, or the way is too rough for our feet. He is very anxious that we shall not fall. If the little lambs fall upon sharp stones, or even in the mud, they get either hurt or dirty. The Good Shepherd wants His lambs white and beautiful."

"Like mine. I wash it every morning, Auntie," said Rose.

"Yes, you are a good little shepherdess. Now, with the little lambs of Jesus, when the cruel stones come or the slippery, ugly mud, a little lamb need only cry out: 'Good Shepherd, pick me up! I can't go any farther unless You carry me!' and, exactly the same way as in Anna's picture, Jesus will place the frightened little lamb upon His shoulders and take it to the safe, beautiful pasture again. And I hope the little lamb, back in the soft green grass, won't forget to say, 'Thank You, Sweet Shepherd, for carrying me over the bad place."

"You mean, Auntie," said Philip thoughtfully, "that sins are our falls, don't you?"

"Yes. Every thought or word or action that we can't be happy to offer the Good Shepherd is some sort of a fall. The little lamb's whiteness is spoiled a bit. The best way is to call out very quickly that we need to be carried. Then we don't fall. If we have been slow, or careless, or maybe simply willful, and have tripped over the rocks or slipped down into the mud, then the Good Shepherd will cure the hurt, will wash away the spot, with His Precious Blood, as soon as we say, 'I'm so sorry! Next time I'll call out in time and not tumble down!' The most wonderful thing about this Good Shepherd is that He gave His life for His sheep. He shed His Precious Blood that His sheep might be saved. There never was such another Shepherd."

"And there never will be, Auntie," said Rose, "because Jesus stays our Shepherd always, doesn't He?"

"Surely. Other shepherds may be faithful and kind, may guard the sheep from danger and trouble, but our Good Shepherd said, 'I lay down My life for My sheep.' It is because we know He died for us that we understand how very, very much He loved us. When we think of Jesus as our Shepherd, we mustn't forget the kind of Shepherd He is. So we say, 'The Good Shepherd'—He is good the way God is good, which is in such a great, wide, grand way that we can't measure the goodness. Anna, here, might as well try to take that high hill, where the sheep are grazing, into her plump little hand as we to try to measure that goodness of Jesus, our Shepherd."

"It's love and kindness, too, isn't it, Auntie?" asked Philip.

"Yes. And unending carefulness. The Shepherd is always looking out for His sheep and His little lambs. Before Jesus ascended into heaven, He had a very solemn talk with His apostles, especially with St. Peter."

"Because," said John, "St. Peter was the chief apostle."

"That is why. Do you know the question Jesus asked St. Peter?"

Rose and Philip looked uncertain. Anna, quite as was to be expected, had fallen asleep.

John gazed thoughtfully across the bright meadows. Something was in his mind about that last talk Jesus had with His apostles. Auntie waited, watching John's face.

"Was it," said he at last, "something about 'Do you love me?'"

"Yes, John. And St. Peter answered the Savior, 'Yes, Lord, you know that I love you.' Now listen to what Jesus, the Good Shepherd, said to St. Peter after that: 'Feed my lambs.'"

"Oh!" cried Rose. "Did He mean us, Auntie?"

"He meant you children, His very little lambs, and us big people, the lambs of the flock, and later Jesus added to St. Peter, 'Feed my sheep.'"

"But who are the sheep, Auntie?" Rose asked.

"The sheep are the bishops and priests, of whom St. Peter was the head. St. Peter was to feed all, from the highest to the lowest and simplest. There is somebody in the world today who is the successor of St. Peter—" Auntie paused.

"Oh, we know!" cried Rose and Philip and John together. "Our Holy Father, the pope, is the successor of St. Peter!"

5

Anna stirred at the shout.

"Hooray!" said she cheerfully, only half-awake.

"Oh, Anna!" said Rose reproachfully.

"That's all right," said Auntie, kissing the flushed face. "I'm glad you were all ready with the answer this time. And, children, this successor of St. Peter has also heard the Good Shepherd say, 'Feed My lambs, feed My sheep.' And, hearing the command of Jesus, the pope has thought particularly of the very little lambs like you. He knows little lambs need food as much as, if not more than, the bigger ones. Little lambs must not be allowed to suffer from hunger just when they need plenty of nourishment in order to grow. Over there on the hillside the little lambs would die if they found no food. So the little lambs of God's flock, the flock of the Good Shepherd, are to be fed, not only with bodily food, but also with the Blessed Food of the soul. The Holy Father says, 'Feed My very little lambs with the Bread of Heaven.'"

"Holy Communion," said John, reverently.

"Holy Communion," repeated Anna, with a baby pronunciation of her very own.

And overhead in the branches of the elm tree, a bird suddenly burst into joyous song.

John's eyes met Auntie's, and the little boy smiled.

"It sounds," he said, "as though the bird knew we were glad."

"Or else as though he wanted to remind Auntie that we mustn't tell all the stories in one morning," laughed Auntie. "Anna has surely heard more than enough, and indeed we all have. Let's remember the Good Shepherd, and stay very close to Him, and tomorrow try to learn some more about Him."

"And I'd like," said Anna, slipping to the ground and taking Auntie's hand invitingly, "to go over to the hill and see the lambs."

So they started off for a walk, Anna leading the little procession by always dancing a trifle ahead of Auntie, whose hand she tightly held.

"Anna jumps around like a lamb, anyway," said Rose.

"Well," said John quickly, "she's gentle like one, too."

"We mustn't forget we are all lambs of the Good Shepherd," said Auntie, "who love one another dearly, who love the Shepherd, and whom He loves with more love than we can put into words."

Then Rose felt ashamed of having felt a wee bit cross about Anna's restlessness, and, running up to the laughing child, she kissed one round cheek.

It was a very happy party that visited the flock upon the hill that day.

Biblical Passages
1. Read the story of the Good Shepherd: John 10:1-15.
2. Read about Jesus' appearance to St. Peter after His Resurrection: John 21:15-17.

Points of Doctrine
1. *Who made the world?* God made the world.
2. *Who is God?* God is the Creator of heaven and earth, and of all things.

3. *What is man?* Man is a creature composed of body and soul, and made to the image and likeness of God.
4. *Why did God make you?* God made me to know Him, to love Him, and to serve Him in this world, and to be happy with Him forever in heaven.

Prayer to Memorize

Because God made all things, including each of us, we offer back to God all that He gives us each day. Every morning, offer your day and yourself to God:

> *My God, I offer up to You*
> *My soul and heart—and my mind too;*
> *And all I do or hear or say*
> *And all my work and all my play.*
> *Amen.*

Younger children may pray a simplified version:

> *My God, I give You myself and my day.*
> *Amen.*

Baptism

WHEN Auntie and the four children paid a visit to the flock upon the hill, something very sweet happened. Rose's little lamb, with the blue ribbon around its neck, ran lovingly toward her to be petted. "See, Auntie!" Rose cried. "I told you it knew me! Oh, you dear, darling little lamb! Don't be cross, mother-sheep! I won't hurt your baby!"

For the mother-sheep had hurried after her baby and, with soft sounds and tender pushes of her nose, was anxiously coaxing it away from Rose. You see, the mother-sheep was jealous.

"Would you know your lamb from the others?" Philip asked.

"N—no," said Rose, who hated to admit that she could not have picked out her pet except for the blue ribbon. "If anyone took off the ribbon, I'd have to wait till the lamb ran to me."

John was caressing every sheep within reach. He was so very gentle that animals never feared him.

"Well," said he, "Auntie, that's the difference about our Lord. He knows His sheep as well as they know Him. Because He is God, and knows everything."

The next morning the group gathered again, under the trees.

"Is this a catechism class?" Philip suddenly asked.

"No, dear. You have that in church, don't you?" Auntie answered. "This is just a little while we spend talking about the great day that is coming: First Communion. We know our catechism pretty well, don't we? Not the big one, of course, but our own simple one made entirely for the littlest lambs. I feel we are away up in that. But we might learn it all the way through beautifully, and at the end find ourselves still very stiff and clumsy about loving our Lord. When He comes to us, we don't want to welcome Him into our souls only with answers out of the catechism, do we?"

Rose burst out laughing.

"No, Auntie. That would be like our company manners, wouldn't it?"

"Very much. Jesus is our Savior, our Best Friend, the Good Shepherd of our soul. We must greet Him by fairly running to Him as the little lamb ran to Rose this morning—'Here I am, dear Shepherd, loving Jesus! Because I studied my catechism, I know You are God, and that You became man for me. And I love You very much, and am glad to receive You into my soul!' We can tell Him about our talks here in the back yard, which we had simply in order to learn to love Him more before He came to us. We can ask Him anything. There is nothing He cannot do."

"And He knows all our names," said John thoughtfully.

"Anna Marie Madeleine," said Anna promptly. "That is mine."

"Yes, He shall call His own by their names, our names given in Holy Baptism, the first sacrament we receive."

"Baptism makes our souls all shining and white,"

said Rose. "Mother said so when our baby brother was baptized."

"The catechism says so, too," said Philip.

"But Mother explained," Rose persisted, "original sin is like a horrid spot, and Baptism washes it off, every bit."

"Nice and clean," Anna added, blinking at a bluebird that blinked back at her from a bough near Auntie's head.

"That's lovely," said Auntie. "And how does Baptism make our souls white and spotless?"

"Through the Precious Blood of Jesus," John replied.

"I thought it was through the water," said Rose uncertainly.

Philip giggled, but Auntie gave him a very decided frown.

"The water is what is used in giving the sacrament. It's the outward sign, the thing we can see," said Auntie. "The grace, which is the washing out of the stain that is upon our souls because Adam and Eve sinned, comes only through the Precious Blood of Jesus."

"I think," said Rose in a very hurt tone, "it's not nice for Philip to laugh at me."

"It's not a bit nice," Auntie agreed; "and Philip means never to do it again. He forgot, that's all. If you children tease one another, our whole time will be wasted, because each one will be afraid to speak out, for fear the others will laugh. Rose did the honest, and the sensible thing, in telling what she thought."

"I'll not laugh any more, Auntie," said Philip, his cheeks very red.

"Thank you, laddie. Baptism makes us children of God, and heirs of heaven, and it also does something of which the blue ribbon around the neck of Rose's lamb made me think."

"What?" asked Philip and Rose eagerly.

"Baptism leaves a mark upon our souls, a mark nothing can ever rub out. So when the Good Shepherd looks upon us, He sees the mark that sets us apart as His property. Rose saw the blue ribbon and she thought, 'My lamb, the one I love best!' No matter in what miserable condition Rose found her lamb, no matter how far from the others, she would say, 'That is my pet lamb, for it wears the blue ribbon I tied about its neck.' So it is with the mark of Baptism. Do as we will, go where we please, our soul shows always that we belong to Jesus Christ, the Good Shepherd, who shed His Precious Blood that His sheep might be saved."

"But if we are very, very wicked afterward, Auntie?" John asked.

"Still there would be the mark of Baptism in our soul. We might be so wicked that people around us would say, 'They can't be Christians. Christians could not be so evil.' And yet our Lord, looking sorrowfully at us would know, 'They are the sheep of My Fold; they belong to Me.' In their soul they carry the mark of Holy Baptism, the mark that is the promise of their salvation unless they willfully choose to be lost."

"We don't choose to be lost," said Philip decidedly.

"I'm going to heaven," declared Anna; "some day."

"If you're good," Rose corrected.

"Of course," said Anna comfortably. "When I get big, I'll never be naughty."

"If you try hard, and keep Jesus in your soul," said Auntie, "you never need be naughty. The question is, how hard will Anna try?"

Anna stared doubtfully at Auntie. Anna loved comfort and petting and doing as she pleased.

"I don't know yet," said Anna at last. "But I'll talk to Jesus about it when my First Communion comes."

With that, Anna threw herself back into Auntie's arms and contentedly watched her friend the bluebird amusing himself looking for insects among the leaves. Auntie kissed Anna's plump, dimpled cheek. All four children were different, and the Good Shepherd would lead each one the way He knew to be the best.

"Nobody could do anything better," said Auntie. "The Good Shepherd will take the best of care of the lambs who always listen for His voice. It's the way of little lambs to follow foolish things, to enter paths not safe for creatures so small and untrained. Then the Good Shepherd calls, 'Come back, stay near Me! I know where you will be safe, and if you listen for My voice, you shall never be alone.' Best of all He tells us, 'I am going to feed you. I intend giving you the Bread of Angels, which is My Body and Blood. Little lambs, prepare your hearts by loving Me as much as you can. Don't be afraid to laugh and play and be very happy. I want you to come to My Feast full of joy.' The Good Shepherd wants a happy flock about Him."

"We're very happy," said John. "It must be terrible not to know about the Good Shepherd."

"Like those who don't believe in God," said Philip.

John gazed far, far off, beyond where the fluffy clouds seemed to touch the tops of the hills.

"Some little boys," said he softly, "are priests when they grow up; and God lets them go to those people who don't know about Him and tell them about the Good Shepherd."

"And," said Rose solemnly, "if the priests get killed when they talk about God, they're martyrs. Aren't they, Auntie?"

"Yes, dear. To die for the Faith our Lord taught is to be a martyr. And, do you know, martyrdom is sometimes called the 'Baptism of Blood.'"

"Yes," said Philip. "I studied about it. If anybody who hasn't been baptized with water should be killed because he believed in Christ, he would be baptized by blood."

"That's splendid. I wonder if any little lamb here can tell Auntie about the third kind of Baptism?"

Rose and John eagerly began together, but in different words, so Auntie put her hands over her ears, crying, "Oh, please, please wait! Rose, you begin, dear."

"It's Baptism of Desire," said Rose. "If you want something terribly, you desire it. And sometimes people have known about Jesus, and never been baptized."

"Then send for the priest," Philip advised.

"Yes," Rose went on, "if there is a priest."

"And if there's no priest, any other person might baptize," Auntie hinted.

Rose's cheeks grew redder in her zeal to explain what Baptism of Desire meant.

"I know, Auntie. But suppose nobody knew how, or nobody would, or the poor thing was dying all alone— then a wish to be baptized would do. Isn't that it?"

"Yes, darling. The heartfelt wish to receive the sacrament would take the place of the Baptism of Water, and in such a case we say the person received the Baptism of Desire. Do all the little lambs understand?"

To Auntie's surprise, it was Anna who inquired, "Would that person with the desire belong to the Good Shepherd, like us?"

"Yes, dear. That person would be as you are through Baptism—the child of God, and heir of heaven, one of the lambs of the Fold of Christ, our Good Shepherd."

Biblical Passages
1. God calls each of us by name. Read Isaiah 43:1.
2. Jesus asked us to teach others about Him and to baptize others in the name of the Blessed Trinity. Read Matthew 28:18-20.

Points of Doctrine
1. *What is a sacrament?* A sacrament is an outward sign instituted by Christ to give grace.
2. *From where do the sacraments get the power to give grace?* The sacraments have the power of giving grace from the merits of Jesus Christ.
3. *What is Baptism?* Baptism is a sacrament that cleanses us from original sin, makes us Christians, children of God, and heirs of heaven.
4. *Is Baptism necessary to salvation?* Baptism is necessary to salvation, because without it we cannot enter into the kingdom of heaven.
5. *Who can administer Baptism?* The priest is the ordinary minister of Baptism; but in case of necessity, anyone who has the use of reason may baptize.
6. *How is Baptism given?* Whoever baptizes should pour water on the head of the person to be baptized,

and say, while pouring the water, *"I baptize you in the name of the Father, and of the Son, and of the Holy Spirit."*

PRAYER TO MEMORIZE

Glory Be

Glory be to the Father,
and to the Son,
and to the Holy Spirit,
As it was in the beginning,
is now, and ever shall be,
world without end.
Amen.

PENANCE

O H, Anna!" cried Rose in a shocked voice, as Auntie and the children took up their usual places for what the little ones had named "Our First Communion Talks." "How could you come in those muddy clothes?"

"I—I tumbled down, and Mother wasn't in the house." Anna was blushing and a little cross at Rose's reproof. "Anyway, I couldn't keep Auntie waiting, could I?" A smile lightened—even chased away—the gloom on the small round face.

Auntie removed a good deal of the dried mud with a convenient handkerchief.

"We'll excuse Anna this time," said Auntie. "I must say the rest of you look wonderfully neat." Auntie's eyes sparkled as she finished her rapid inspection of the children. "I'm glad you think it right to be quite in order for our talks."

"It's out of respect, isn't it?" Rose asked.

"Reverence," John added very softly.

"Yes, reverence," Auntie smiled at John. "Things must fit, you know."

"I was making mud pies," Anna declared quickly, again offended by an disapproving glance Rose threw at her still soiled clothes. "And nobody can, and stay clean!"

"Nobody can," Auntie agreed. "So nobody expects anybody to be spotless after playing with mud. But what is quite suitable for mud pies would be very much out-of-place at school, or at church, or to go visiting."

"Or," said Philip decidedly, "to wear at First Communion talks."

Anna was upon the verge of tears. Auntie's comforting kiss came barely in time.

"We know that, and we need not be told again," said Auntie, so seriously that Philip dropped his eyes. "And we are nicely started upon a splendid subject for today. It's funny how often some simple, perhaps even some rather unpleasant, thing that happens in the early morning will give us enough to think about all day. The little lambs have themselves given Auntie her subject this morning. The muddy clothes made everybody feel that certain things are out-of-place at certain times. Not that the muddy clothes of themselves are dreadful: not at all. Mud pies necessarily mean muddy clothes. It's only that things must fit. Another way of saying the same thing is, 'Things must be suitable for the circumstances about them.' I'm sure you all hear a great deal about order, don't you?"

"Yes," sighed Rose; "I think I hear about order a million times every day."

"And you never keep anything in order," said Philip severely, "because Mother says so."

Auntie spoke before Rose could answer:

"It's not in order, Philip, for you to correct Rose. This seems to be a day when the little lambs are not so loving and lovable as they might be. Wouldn't it be awful if the Good Shepherd would love them less, too?"

"Oh, dear!" groaned Anna. "I want Him to love me!"

"He does love you. Remember, Jesus is always the Good Shepherd, even if we are sometimes very naughty lambs. He never will stop loving His flock. Knowing how He loves us, don't we want to please Him?"

"Of course we do, Auntie," John answered.

"We want to," said Auntie, "and yet, sometimes we don't. We get out of order. You see, to keep in order we must always obey our Good Shepherd. When we disobey, we sin, and sin can never be anything but disorder." Auntie paused, certain John had something to say. There was a look of deep thought upon the boy's face.

"If anything is in disorder, it's upset," he said gravely.

"Yes," said Auntie.

"And if," said John, "we do anything wrong, we do get upset, Auntie."

"I broke a glass this morning," said Anna suddenly.

"Did you tell your mother?" Philip quickly asked.

"Not yet," said Anna faintly. "I—I'm going to."

"If you don't tell," said Rose, "your mother will think someone else did it."

"Anna is going to tell," said John. "She'll tell as soon as Mommy comes home from the village."

"Of course," said Anna, tossing her curly head at the others while she smiled bravely at her brother. "I've hardly seen Mommy at all yet today."

"Mommy will know it was only an accident," said Auntie cheerfully, "and Anna is learning to be more careful all the time."

"She breaks an awful lot," said Rose.

"If she does," said Auntie, "she may be the one to say so. The best way is to tell as soon as we can when we have done what was wrong, or careless, or ungrateful. The worst way to treat our Good Shepherd is to turn our faces away from Him because we have fallen into some fault. It is strange, but very often after we know we have disobeyed Him—after we have gone a step away from Him—instead of turning quickly and asking to be forgiven, we run far away like cowards. Perhaps it is because we forget how gentle and loving the Good Shepherd is—how willingly He forgives us, puts us in order again—and we are afraid; or perhaps pride catches hold of us and we don't want to face the Good Shepherd and admit we have offended Him. In either case, we go sadly astray. I think the most unbecoming fault for the Good Shepherd's lambs is pride. Little lambs—see them over there upon the hillside—are timid, untrained creatures, who can never be too near the Good Shepherd, listening for the sound of His guiding voice."

As Auntie spoke, the Scotch collie dog who was watching the sheep gave a number of short, angry barks.

"Bow-wow-wow!" mimicked Anna gleefully. "Oh, he's awfully angry, Auntie! See him rushing after that poor little lamb by the stone fence!"

All the children turned to watch Bruce unmistakably scolding the little lamb that had strayed from its mother.

"He says," Anna went on, "'Go back, go back, little-bit-o'-lamb! Go back where you belong!'"

"And he has done his work," Auntie finished with a laugh. "The little lamb has turned and gone back. That's the way conscience does with us. Conscience is the watch-dog that barks when we are in danger of going out of the way proper for lambs of the Good Shepherd. We must ask for very strong, clever watch-dogs, in the way of consciences. They are a great help."

"But sometimes," said John, with a troubled face, "we are not like that little lamb; we don't go back when our conscience barks at us."

"Very true," said Auntie. "Still, the Good Shepherd is waiting for us, and waiting with a remedy. You know He died for His sheep. He will not let them be lost, unless they insist upon refusing salvation. Now we get back to the fact that things must fit. We are going to receive Holy Communion; we are going to welcome Jesus, our Good Shepherd, into our souls. Then our souls must be free from sin; they must be clean and in order when Jesus comes. He gave us the robe of baptismal innocence; the question is, have we kept that robe spotless? Possibly we have—perhaps we have not. Anyway, our Good Shepherd has left us among the seven sacraments, the Sacrament of Penance, the sure means of making our souls all white and beautiful, like the souls of little babies just baptized."

"The Sacrament of Penance is confession," said Philip.

"To confess our sins to the priest of God is part of the Sacrament of Penance—the part that belongs especially to us. The priest gives us the absolution, or the forgiveness, speaking for God Himself."

"The way Mother sends messages by me sometimes?" Rose asked. "Once she let me take so many to Auntie Nelson, who was ill."

"Something like that. The priest gives us a penance, too, generally some extra prayer to offer God in loving atonement for our sins against Him. But simply to tell our faults would not be doing all that is necessary upon our part."

"I know," said John; "we must be sorry—awfully sorry."

"And," Philip added, "we must mean never to be so wicked anymore."

21

Rose cast an anxious glance at Auntie.

"Suppose we're not awfully sorry?" the child asked.

"You will be, dear," said Auntie, "if you stop to remember. The Good Shepherd died to open heaven for us. He wants us—oh, more than we shall understand until we are safely there at home with Him—to be the true lambs of His fold! Sin is the only thing that can keep us away from Him. We don't any of us want to be away from Him, do we?"

"No, indeed," said the four together—Anna a trifle less promptly than the others. Her attention would wander to the clouds and the flowers, and to whatever passed over the hill she could see from her place in the yard.

"Sometimes we may be afraid we aren't sorry enough," Auntie continued, "but then we must ask ourselves if we wouldn't wish not to have offended our Good Shepherd Who laid down His life for His sheep? I am quite sure we shall never be able to look at Him dying for us without crying out, 'I am sorry I was so wicked and ungrateful, Jesus, Good Shepherd, not just because wicked people must be punished so terribly, but because I really love You.'"

"That's like the Act of Contrition," said Philip.

"Yes, the Act of Contrition we say while the priest gives us absolution—the first part is like what I said. To make it very short, for the Good Shepherd's very little lambs, it may be simply, 'I am sorry, Lord Jesus, because I love You'; and the second part, that important part that shows we mean to work hard in the future to please our Good Shepherd, may be just, 'Help me not to offend You again.'"

"We have to learn an Act of Contrition," said Philip; "I like that short one. Will you teach it to us, Auntie?"

"Surely." Auntie caught John's smile. "Do you know it, John?"

"I think so."

"Say it for us."

"I am sorry, Lord Jesus, because I love You; help me not to offend You again.'"

"Not to 'fend You again,'" Anna echoed, her hands solemnly clasped.

"Very good," said Auntie. "And after confession, after the Precious Blood—because only the Precious Blood gives power to the sacraments—has made our souls white and beautiful again, we are fit to go very near the Good Shepherd. More than that, we are prepared to receive Him into our souls."

A moment's quiet settled upon the group under the elm tree.

"Into our souls," said John afterwards. "They ought to be very beautiful, Auntie, oughtn't they?"

"Yes—as beautiful as we can make them."

"We're going to try," said Philip.

"We're going to try hard," said John.

"Auntie," Rose whispered, "Anna didn't fall asleep today."

"Of course not," said Anna indignantly; "I'm listening for my own First Communion, too."

"You don't always—" Rose began. Then she blushed brightly and stopped. "We're going to try hard," she finished, and she blushed again at Auntie's brilliant, approving smile.

Biblical Passages

1. On the necessity of Baptism, read John 3:5-6.
2. On the necessity of confessing our sins to a priest, read John 20:19-23.

Points of Doctrine

1. *What is the Sacrament of Penance?* Penance is a sacrament in which the sins committed after Baptism are forgiven.
2. *What must we do to receive the Sacrament of Penance worthily?* To receive the Sacrament of Penance worthily, we must do five things:
    i. We must examine our conscience.
    ii. We must have sorrow for our sins.
    iii. We must make a firm resolution never more to offend God.
    iv. We must confess our sins to the priest.
    v. We must accept the penance which the priest gives us.
3. *What is contrition?* Contrition, or sorrow for sin, is a hatred of sin and true grief of the soul for having offended God, with a firm purpose of sinning no more.
4. *What is confession?* Confession is the telling of our sins to a duly authorized priest, for the purpose of obtaining forgiveness.
5. *Why does the priest give us a penance after confession?* The priest gives us a penance after confession

that we may satisfy God for the temporal punishment due to our sins.

PRAYER TO MEMORIZE

Act of Contrition

O my God, I am heartily sorry for having offended Thee.
I detest all my sins, because of Thy just punishments,
but most of all because they offend Thee, my God,
who art all-good and deserving of all my love.
I firmly resolve, with the help of Thy grace,
to sin no more and to avoid the near occasions of sin.
Amen.

Shorter Act of Contrition

I am sorry, Lord Jesus, because I love You;
help me not to offend You again.
Amen.

Obedience

T HERE had been quite some excitement among the flock of sheep upon the hill; and the children were flushed and eager when they gathered about Auntie in the back yard.

"It wasn't my lamb, Auntie," Rose explained. "At first I thought it was, but when the boy picked it up I saw it hadn't a blue ribbon around its neck."

"It's all bloody," Anna cheerfully announced; "it's fur —no, wool—" as Philip giggled—"is torn just awfully, and its mother—she cried, Auntie, she really did!"

"The lamb was jammed between two stones," grave John went on. "If it had stayed with its mother, it would not have rolled down among the loose rocks."

"Stayed by its mother," Anna most solemnly repeated, "and did as it was told." She rolled her eyes at everybody in turn.

"Like we children have to do," said Rose.

"Not stay by our mothers, we boys," said Philip indignantly. "We're not girls!"

"I like to stay with my mother," Rose declared with a very superior air.

"And Philip does, too," said Auntie, speaking for the first time. "But Philip means that both boys and girls who are worth anything may be trusted to do the right thing, even when Mother is not present."

John, who had been thinking earnestly, raised his eyes to Auntie's face. "The little lamb that was crushed didn't know any better," said he.

"That's the point, John," Auntie agreed. "And it's the point for us. Not being able to know everything, we need to be guided and controlled—especially while we are small children. God has given us the Church, our priests, our teachers. Why?"

The older children hesitated. John parted his lips, then blushed and kept silent. Auntie was about to encourage him, for John was often too shy to speak out, when Anna suddenly said, "To make us mind."

"To make us obedient," Rose corrected, because Rose knew ever so many more words than little Anna.

"Means the same," said Anna, not at all pleased at Rose's attempt to improve her remark.

"Yes, it does," said Auntie. "We are bound to obey God and His Church, our parents and our teachers, and the rulers God places over our country."

"That's keeping the law, isn't it?" Philip asked.

"Yes, Philip. Obedience is a noble, a heavenly virtue; no disobedience could remain in heaven. The angels obey God always."

"The angels that disobeyed are with Satan, aren't they?" John asked.

"They were put out of heaven forever, with their leader, whom we now call Satan. They are in hell, the place of punishment that will never, never end. We must not forget that they are in that awful place because they would not obey. God hates disobedience as much as He loves obedience."

"I hate vinegar as much as I love sugar," said Anna.

"You mustn't love things to eat," said Rose.

"Anna means," Auntie interfered, "that she understands what I mean."

"Of course," said Anna, closing her eyes with a sigh of satisfaction.

"Now we saw how getting away from its mother's guidance ended with that poor little lamb. You see, the mother is older, and wiser and stronger, and the poor little lamb needed to keep quite close to her. The mother would have shown the safe, sure way down the hill."

"The little lamb should have watched and followed," said Philip.

"Quite so. Somebody must show the way, and that somebody for the little lamb is its mother."

"Little children must follow their mothers, too," said Rose.

"Little children must learn to obey. It is a wonderful thing to be allowed to obey. Suppose God had put us here in this big world and left us to find our own way as best we could?"

"Then," said John, "I suppose, Auntie, we'd get into worse trouble than the poor little lamb."

"We surely should. Our Good Shepherd did not treat us in that fashion. He gave us our Church and our parents, and His beautiful teachings. He provided for every want of His flock. He has told us what we must do, and what we must not dare do, and He has left us our safety in obedience. We look up to everyone wiser and better than we. God is wisest and best of all. Are we unwilling to be led by Him Who knows everything, Who created us, Who understands our dangers, and Who wants to keep us always safe? God Himself is back of all real authority. You obey your parents because God has said you must. Once in a while, a child feels ashamed to obey. 'I'm so big, why can't I do as I please?' he thinks. Then if he obeys at all, it's in a sulky, ugly fashion. But think of obeying because God Himself has commanded! Could there be any greater, any prouder duty, for little lambs, than obedience to our Heavenly Father?"

"Mother once told us," said Rose eagerly, "that men were proud of taking orders from a great general, but that we might be prouder of taking orders from God."

"And when Jesus came on earth," John added, "He showed us how to obey, by obeying the Blessed Mother."

"Yes," said Auntie, "Our Good Shepherd, living in this world as a little Child, obeyed always and at once, His Blessed Mother, Mary."

"He didn't," said Philip, glancing at Rose, "say, 'Why?' or 'Must I?'"

"He just went and did it," said Anna very seriously. She did not look at Rose. Anna was thinking how very hard it was to obey "at once."

Auntie noticed the earnest expression upon Anna's face. "It's harder for some to obey than it is for others," Auntie said. "And the Good Shepherd understands."

Anna brightened.

"The harder it is, the more we need to ask Him to help us, and the more He will love us for trying," Auntie went on.

"Sometimes," said Philip, "we don't want to try."

"That's it," Auntie agreed. "God gave us our will for our very own. We don't have to serve the Good Shepherd unless we choose. We are His children, not His slaves."

"But who wouldn't choose?" John asked. "He has done so much for us, Auntie!"

"And we love to be His little lambs," declared Anna.

"We are glad to live in the sheepfold of the Good Shepherd," said Auntie. "We are happy and thankful beyond words that He will keep us good, strong lambs to do His Will, by feeding us with the Bread of Life, His Body and Blood in Holy Communion. If we had no Shepherd, we should grow weak, starve, and die."

"You mean our souls would die, Auntie?" Rose asked.

"Yes, dear. By dead souls we mean lost souls—souls that can never see God. Jesus comes to us in order to strengthen us, to keep us from sin, to help us in our journey towards heaven. He does not need us, but oh, we need Him dreadfully! And He has promised to stay with us. Now a beautiful way to show we appreciate the love that makes Him come to us and remain with us is to be always obedient to those God in His wisdom has placed over us. The Good Shepherd loves obedience very dearly. It is especially the virtue of Jesus Himself. He was, above all else, obedient. In the Bible, God's Book—the Book better than all other books put together —we are told that Jesus 'became obedient unto death.'"

"What does that mean, Auntie?" asked Rose.

"It means that Jesus, during His whole life upon this earth, obeyed His Heavenly Father. You all know how that life ended."

"On the Cross," said Philip, "where He died for all men."

"To open heaven for them," Rose added.

"Because," said John, "no soul that is stained by sin can enter heaven, and the Precious Blood washes away the sins of the world."

"That is very well explained," said Auntie, pleased that the little lambs were able to tell her so much. "Really you often surprise me."

"Why, Auntie!" Rose exclaimed. "We know only a very little."

"But," said John, "although we know only a very little, we know it about terribly big things, don't we, Auntie?"

"Yes, indeed. Here we are in the back yard under the old elm tree—four little people and one not-so-very-big Auntie—yet we can know about the great God, and can learn to love Him because we know Him, and obey Him because we love Him."

"He is the Good Shepherd as well as the great God," said John.

"If we knew Him only through His greatness as God," said Auntie, "we might be afraid of Him; we might suppose that we must fall upon our knees and hide our faces and tremble. But we know Him as God-become-man in the Second Person of the Blessed Trinity; we know Him as the tender, loving Shepherd, who lived in this world to show men how they should live. We know He despised no one, not even those who had gone far astray. We know Him above all as the Blessed Sacrament upon our altars. And instead of covering our faces and trembling, we look up to see Him inviting us to come nearer—more than that—commanding us to receive Him into our souls. We hear Him call us His sheep for whom He laid down His life, and we are not afraid to go to Him after that. It is a sweet thought that we receive Him in Holy Communion through obedience. What did He say? 'Come to Me, all.' We go by invitation. Jesus, the Host, the Sacred Host, wants us. He has prepared a Feast and asked us to it. We need not be very old, or very clever, or even grown up. He has told us to come, so long as we know Whom we receive."

"Jesus Christ," said John reverently, "true God and true man."

"Jesus Who 'became obedient unto death' for us," said Auntie. "Wouldn't it be very shabby for us upon our side to refuse to obey Him?"

"Indeed it would," answered all the children.

"So we'll ask Him to make us faithful, to teach us to obey as beautifully as He obeyed the Blessed Mother. We shall never obey crossly, complainingly; we'll obey gladly, generously, to please our Good Shepherd Who has taught us by His own example how to make obedience perfect."

For a whole minute, the children were still. The little lambs were thinking of Jesus obeying Mary, His mother. He was coming to them. From Him they could learn the sort of obedience that love makes sweet. They meant to try hard not to be stupid at this lesson. It was one of the lessons that Jesus loved very much. And He Himself, the Good Shepherd, would be the Teacher of His little lambs.

Biblical Passages

1. Read Luke 2:51 on Jesus' obedience to His parents.
2. Jesus calls all to come to Him: Matthew 11:28-30.
3. "Obedient unto death"—See Philippians 2:8.
4. "Not slaves but friends"—See John 15:14-15.

Points of Doctrine

1. *What are angels?* Angels are bodiless spirits created to adore and enjoy God in heaven.
2. *What is hell?* Hell is a state to which the wicked are condemned, and in which they are deprived of the sight of God for all eternity, and are in dreadful torments.
3. *What is heaven?* Heaven is the state of everlasting life in which we see God face to face, are made like unto Him in glory, and enjoy eternal happiness.
4. *What is actual sin?* Actual sin is any willful thought, word, deed, or omission contrary to the law of God. It is disobedience to God's laws.
5. *What is Holy Communion?* Holy Communion is the receiving of the Body and Blood of Christ.

Prayer to Memorize

Our Father (Lord's Prayer)

Our Father, who art in heaven,
Hallowed be Thy name;
Thy kingdom come;
Thy will be done on earth as it is in heaven.
Give us this day our daily bread;
And forgive us our trespasses as we forgive those
who trespass against us;
And lead us not into temptation,
But deliver us from evil. Amen.

ThE Holy ChildHood

"IT seems to me," Auntie began, helping Anna to
climb into her lap, "that as we were talking about
obedience yesterday, the very best thing for us to talk
about next will be the Childhood of Jesus."

"He lived with Mary and Joseph at Nazareth," said
Philip.

"Nazareth was in Galilee." Rose was proud that she
knew.

"It was a very small house," John said, "and the Holy
Family was poor."

"Very poor," said Auntie. "Everybody worked hard."

"Baby Jesus, too?" asked Anna.

"Baby Jesus as soon as He was old enough. You see,
our dear Lord, our Good Shepherd, came as a tiny Baby
and grew older and bigger like other children. As He
lay in the Blessed Mother's arms, the people going by
did not know that the Child His Mother held so tenderly was the Son of God and God Himself."

"Second Person of the Blessed Trinity," said Philip.

"There are three Persons in the Blessed Trinity,"
said Anna, "Father, Son and Holy Spirit." She lisped a
little, and sing-songed a lot, but Anna was sure of her
knowledge. She had once asked questions for a solid
hour about "one God in three divine Persons"—and she
would never again become confused. There was one God
in three Persons. Mother had given her a rose and said,

"That is a single rose; it makes itself known to you by its color, its form, and its perfume. But it is not three roses, is it?" And Anna had realized that Mother was right; Anna held one rose in her hand, not three; yet she would have known the whole rose by means of any of its manifestations.

"Yes," said Auntie, "God the Father, God the Son, and God the Holy Spirit are the three Persons of the Blessed Trinity. Our human minds can't fully understand this mystery of the three Persons, but it is one of the truths we know by faith. In Ireland, St. Patrick taught the mystery to the people by showing them the shamrock, which is made up of three tiny leaves, formed something like our clover, upon one stem. Examples like that are the best we can use to help us understand in a dim way the existence of the Holy Trinity. And every time we make the Sign of the Cross, we profess our faith in the three Persons. You know we say 'In the Name'—never Names, as though there were several—of the Father, Son and Holy Spirit.' That means 'In the Name of One God, Who exists in three divine Persons, the Father, the Son and the Holy Spirit.' By the Sign of the Cross, too, we show that Jesus, the Second Person of the Blessed Trinity, became man and died for our sins."

"Because," said Philip, "God could not die, as God alone."

"No, Jesus had to become man in order to die. Most of the people who saw Him at Nazareth thought He was only man."

"If they had known He was God," said John, "they would not have walked past the house without stopping; they would have waited to kneel down and adore Him."

"The shepherds who heard the angels sing when Christ was born, the Wise Men who travelled miles and miles to find Him and offer their gifts—these knew that the Child in the Holy House at Nazareth was the Son of God. The Blessed Mother and St. Joseph knew. Besides these, the priest Simeon and the holy widow Anna had known when Jesus was presented in the Temple. The Blessed Mother's cousin, St. Elizabeth, recognized the divine Child, too, but altogether there were only a few people in the whole world who understood that the Son of God was with Mary and Joseph at Nazareth."

"Plenty of people don't know He is in the tabernacle now," said Rose. "I'm glad I do." The little girl's eyes shone.

"They need only believe what He said," said Auntie, "at the Last Supper when He instituted the Sacrament of the Eucharist, which we call the Blessed Sacrament, because it is Jesus Himself. All seven sacraments are holy, but Holy Eucharist is the Sacrament of Sacraments. It gives us not merely grace, as every sacrament gives; it gives us the Author of Grace—our Lord Himself. There is something very sad in the thought that so many pass by Jesus in the Blessed Sacrament uncaring, because unknowing, like the people of Nazareth."

"The angels knew Him at Nazareth," said John.

"And they know Him now upon the altar," said Rose.

"And when we go into church, there are more angels—" began Anna. Philip interrupted her by a loud laugh.

"Oh, Anna! You're not an angel!" he cried.

Anna flushed.

"I didn't say I was," said she, much offended. "If you weren't a rude boy, you'd wait till I had finished. Wouldn't he, Auntie?"

"Philip was thoughtless," soothed Auntie.

"I mean," said Anna, with a most aggrieved toss of her curls in Philip's direction, "that our guardian angels are with us, and so there are more angels in the church while we are there."

"Quite right," agreed Auntie, as Philip's teasing died in embarrassed silence. "And isn't it a sort of comforting thought that our guardian angels are with us, to help us adore Jesus in the Blessed Sacrament? They are certain to behave properly, and we may hope they make up for our mistakes. The angels surrounded Jesus at Nazareth, too. They adored the helpless little Child in the Blessed Mother's arms. They knew He was the King of Kings and that He accepted littleness and helplessness by choice. He could have come as a great earthly King, had He so willed. While He was very young, the Blessed Mother cared for Him; as He grew, He began to help her at her work. He was never lazy, never too tired to be of use."

"St. Joseph was a carpenter," said Philip; "we have a picture of him with the Child Jesus carrying some wood."

"It's a very sweet picture," said Auntie. "I think one point you ought to make clear to yourselves at First Communion is that you intend not to waste your time. The smallest of you can do something useful every day. If you look at our Good Shepherd as a little Child, helping the Blessed Mother and St. Joseph, you will be rather ashamed to be always idle."

"I can't do anything," said Anna, in a distressed tone; "besides, I don't want to."

"Just because you don't like to," said Auntie, "whatever you do will be very dear to Jesus. Shut your eyes a minute and think of Him working in the Holy House. He was working for you and me. He wants us to be like Him. Suppose as the divine Child was carrying the wood to St. Joseph, you had been there and He turned to you and said, 'Anna, I am living for you, and I am going to suffer and die for you. Is there any little thing you would be glad to do for Me?'"

Anna's eyes were tightly closed. When she opened them after a minute, to Auntie's surprise there were tears upon the long lashes.

"I," Anna pulled Auntie's head down and whispered into her ear, "could keep my toys in order for Him."

"That's a fine idea. You see, every single one of us can do something. And let's do it every day. Looking at the Child Jesus, we find Him faithful to everything He begins. We are likely to begin heaps of things, but oh dear! We give so many of them up! We need to ask our Good Shepherd, Who never stops looking after us, to help us keep on after we start. To work, to be brave at what we mean to do, He teaches us from the Holy House at Nazareth. Nobody was lazy there, nobody wasted any time."

"And nobody was cross," said Rose.

"Nobody was ever cross. Every word that was spoken was gentle and loving. Little children are forming habits constantly. Many of these habits they are forming are nothing but copies of what they see older people doing. Now it's an excellent thing to have a model, provided the model is a good one. Where can little lambs find not simply a good model, but the one perfect Model?"

"Oh, I know!" Philip answered. "In the Holy House at Nazareth, the Child Jesus was the perfect Model."

"Exactly. The Child Jesus was industrious—which means fond of work and faithful to it—obedient, gentle and helpful. That Child Jesus was our Good Shepherd, Who feeds His lambs with the Holy Communion. When He comes to you, dear little ones, for the first time, be sure to tell Him you thank Him for His Holy Childhood. Tell Him you want to be as much as you can like He was at Nazareth. Say to Him you'd like to be of use in His beautiful world. Above all else, ask Him to keep you from every sin. You know He loves the little lambs of His flock in a special way; ask Him to make you understand how dear you are to Him, and to teach you to love Him with your whole hearts. Loving Jesus in the Blessed Sacrament is the easiest way to keep sweet and patient no matter what happens. Is He not patient there, in the little white Host? He is always ready, always waiting for you. The tabernacle is small, like the Holy House at Nazareth; Jesus was the little Child there, He is the little Host here. Why was He the Child, why is He the Sacred Host?"

"Because He loves us," John answered.

"Because He loves us," the others echoed.

Biblical Passages

Re-read the story of our beloved Savior's birth in St. Luke, chapter 2.

Points of Doctrine

1. *What is the Blessed Trinity?* The Blessed Trinity is one God in three divine Persons.
2. *Are the three divine Persons one and the same God?* The three divine Persons are one and the same God, having one and the same divine nature.
3. *What do you believe of Jesus Christ?* I believe that Jesus Christ is the son of God, the second Person of the Blessed Trinity, true God and true man.
4. *What is the Holy Eucharist (Blessed Sacrament)?* The Holy Eucharist is the sacrament which contains the Body, Blood, Soul, and Divinity,of our Lord Jesus Christ under the appearances of bread and wine.
5. *What do you mean by the appearances of bread and wine?* By the appearances of bread and wine, I mean the figure, the color, the taste, and whatever appears to the senses.

Prayer to Memorize

Prayer to My Guardian Angel

Angel of God, my guardian dear,
To whom God's love entrusts me here,
Ever this day be at my side,
To light and guard, to rule and guide. Amen.

Or:

Prayer to St. Joseph

Most pure Spouse of the Virgin Mary,
pray for us daily to the Son of God,
that armed with the weapons of His grace,
we may fight as we ought in this life,
and be crowned by Him in death.
Amen.

Children of Mary

BRIGHT faces greeted Auntie the day after she and the children had talked about the Holy Childhood. "I should judge," said Auntie mischievously, "that you four small children had been extremely good since yesterday. You all look so shiningly happy."

A guilty laugh rippled out under the elm tree.

"I was good," said Anna simply. "I did everything Mommy wanted—and everything Father told me."

The others laughed again. They felt too big to tell what Anna did not mind telling. Auntie's guess had been perfectly correct. The four children had carefully tried to be as much as possible like the Child Jesus. Although the three older ones would not praise themselves, they were glad Auntie knew.

"It's easier when we look at the Child Jesus," said Auntie. "Although you are all still really small children, you're not too little to begin to think, just for a moment every morning, of the Model you mean to copy: The Child Jesus at home with the Blessed Mother."

"And to say we'll do everything during the day for Him," said Rose.

"And ask His mother to help us," said Philip.

"That will be splendid," said Auntie. "Imagine how glad that dear mother will be to help you to grow like her Son! She knew Jesus better than anyone else could know Him, so she can show us the way to copy Him, best of all. Mary never forgot her divine Son for one instant."

"She must watch us all very much now," said John thoughtfully, "while we are getting ready to receive Him in Holy Communion."

"Yes. You are preparing to receive her Child. Mary was the first in the whole world to receive Him, when He came, a tiny Baby—she welcomed Him with her heart simply full of perfect love for Him. Oh, we can learn more than we can measure from that love of the Blessed Mother for the Child Jesus! And think what an honor it is for us, that we are Mary's children, too."

"Are we really?" asked Anna, her attention suddenly caught by this idea.

"Surely. You and I, and all Christians in the entire world are children of Mary. In that way, Jesus is our elder Brother, as well as our Good Shepherd."

"He is our Brother," said John, "because His mother is our mother, too."

"I wonder," said Auntie, "if any one remembers when Mary became our mother?"

The children considered. They knew they called her "The Blessed Mother," yet for the moment no one could think why the mother of Jesus was the mother of all Christians, too.

"Well," began Auntie, "the answer has something to do with Good Friday."

John's face lighted up.

"'At the Cross her station keeping,'" he said, "'stood the mournful mother weeping.'"

Rose and Philip finished with him: "'Close to Jesus to the last.'"

"Very good," said Auntie. "You all know that Mary stood by the Cross of her Son. You know, too, that Jesus spoke from the Cross seven different times."

"Oh!" cried Philip. "I know, Auntie—our Lord said to St. John from the Cross, 'Behold thy Mother.'"

The others sighed their satisfaction. It was so comforting to have one of their group know things!

"That's right," said Auntie. "Wasn't it something very solemn to be told, just before Jesus died? When we call Mary our Blessed Mother, let's sometimes stop and think where she was given that name. Where did Jesus die?"

"On Calvary," answered Rose.

"And on Calvary, while He was dying, He gave us Mary for our mother. After Himself, she was the best gift Jesus could give us. His mother, the holiest of God's creatures, the one chosen to care for God's own Son, was made the mother of us poor sinners."

"We are terribly different from the Child Jesus," sighed Rose.

"So different," said Auntie, "that I wonder that the Blessed Mother accepted us. Yet she did. And do you know why? She saw, standing there by the Cross at Calvary, how much her divine Son suffered for love of us. She learned how extremely dear we are to Him, how precious are our souls that were bought by the Precious Blood."

"The Blessed Mother found out," said Rose, "what Jesus paid for us."

"Yes. If you were given a handful of diamonds and were told they cost two million dollars, would you dare throw them away?"

"Of course not," replied the four children.

"That is because you know that two million dollars is a great deal of money; you value the diamonds because of what they cost. But what all the world could give you, piled up higher than mountains and reaching out more broadly than the seas, could not be worth one human soul—Why?"

"Because," said John, "it took the Precious Blood to buy our souls."

"And our Blessed Mother knows the price. So she could not refuse us. We were worth too much to her divine Son. Our Good Shepherd did indeed give His life for us, His sheep, and He gave it in the presence of Mary, His mother. She counted the cost, there upon Calvary, my dear little lambs, and she knows how valuable we are."

"I wonder she stayed there," said Rose, "watching Jesus die."

"Mothers always stay," declared Anna gravely. "My mommy stayed when my throat was cut."

"Your throat wasn't cut," said Rose. "It was only something in your throat."

"Well," said Anna, "Mommy stayed anyway. And mothers always stay."

"So they do," Auntie heartily agreed. "A mother's love and a mother's patience are enormous. It's the strong love of a mother's heart that gives her courage to suffer anything for her child. The Blessed Mother's love was the most perfect that could be, and that is why her courage was so great. She did not run away while they were crucifying her Son; she did not faint or hide her face. She stood bravely until the end, made strong through her great love."

"And she was brave, too," said John, "to take us for her children."

"Some of us," said Philip very seriously, "are a disgrace to her."

"Oh, I hope not any of us here," cried Auntie. "We want to be a comfort to her, don't we?"

"Yes, we do," answered the three older children.

"I think so," added Anna.

"And she likes our goodwill. You know how your earthly mothers smile when you try to be good; how they pet you and seem to love you even more than usual. Now think of the Blessed Mother's smile when you try to copy her Son. Do you suppose she could forget Calvary?"

"Oh, no!" cried Rose. "It was too dreadful!"

"Neither can she forget that it was there she became our mother. We may call upon her, certain that she will hear and help us. We may ask her to teach us the ways of the Child Jesus. At this time, you little ones ought to beg her over and over again to prepare you to welcome her Son in Holy Communion. No one else understands so well how to meet the Lord Jesus, our Good Shepherd. Ask her to watch over you day and night, and when First Communion morning comes, to take you to the altar."

"That will be beautiful, Auntie," said John softly, "to have the Blessed Mother beside us."

"Ask her to be there," said Auntie with a bright smile at John, "and you may be sure she will not refuse."

"Our fathers and mothers come," said Rose, "and grandfathers and grandmothers. And we may invite Jesus' mother, too."

"You may, and you all do. Don't you?" asked Auntie.

"Yes, indeed, Auntie," came the answer.

"Then she will help to make your First Communion day the most beautiful day of your lives. You will receive Jesus not only in the company of angels, but with the Queen of the Angels beside you. All through your lives, she will help you remember that she, the Mother of Jesus, took you to the altar and gave you to her Son as His little brothers and sisters, because she had adopted you as her children, and you did not forget to invite her to your First Communion.

"The Good Shepherd must be especially glad to welcome little lambs who come to Him in the care of His mother. And now, before we part this morning, let us say one 'Remember, O Most Glorious Virgin Mary' for a happy, loving, blessed First Communion."

Anna slipped from Auntie's lap to the ground. Then they knelt down in the soft grass under the elm tree, Auntie and the four children, and not even a single little bird made a sound while they said the prayer together.

Biblical Passages

1. Read John 19:25-27—Jesus gives us His mother.
2. Read the seven last words of Jesus: Luke 23:34 and 43, John 19:26-27, Mark 15:34, John 19:28 and 30, and Luke 23:46.

Points of Doctrine

1. *Was anyone ever preserved from the stain of original sin?* The Blessed Virgin Mary, through the merits of her divine Son, was preserved free from the guilt of original sin, and this privilege is called her Immaculate Conception.
2. *Is the Blessed Virgin Mary truly the Mother of God?* The Blessed Virgin Mary is truly the Mother of God, because the same divine Person who is the son of God is also the Son of the Blessed Virgin Mary.
3. *Why did Christ suffer and die?* Christ suffered and died for our sins.
4. *What lessons do we learn from the sufferings and death of Christ?* From the sufferings and death of Christ, we learn the great evil of sin, the hatred God bears to it, and the necessity of satisfying for it.

Prayer to Memorize

Hail Mary

Hail Mary, full of grace!
The Lord is with thee;
blessed art thou among women,
and blessed is the fruit of thy womb, Jesus.
Holy Mary, Mother of God,
pray for us sinners,
now and at the hour of our death.
Amen.

Or:

Memorare

Remember, O most gracious Virgin Mary,
that never was is know that anyone who

fled to thy protection, implored thy help, or
sought thy intercession was left unaided.
Inspired by this confidence I fly to thee,
O Virgin of virgins, my mother.
To thee do I come, before thee I stand,
sinful and sorrowful.
O Mother of the Word Incarnate,
Despise not my petitions, but in thy mercy,
Hear and answer me.
Amen.

Faith

"PHILIP is not back from the village yet, Auntie," said Rose. "We'll have to wait."

"Yes; we don't care to begin until we are all here, do we?"

"He may not come, though, for a long time," Rose objected.

"Yes, he'll come very soon," said John. "You know Philip is always on time."

"He wasn't the day his pony ran away and threw him into the ditch," pouted Rose.

"Philip couldn't help that," explained John.

"He was all hurt on his head," sighed Anna. "Poor Philip!"

"I mean," said John patiently, "that Philip is never late if he can help it. I know he will be here directly."

Auntie looked thoughtfully at John's decided face.

"How do you know?" she asked suddenly.

"Wh—why, Auntie," answered John, a little confused, "I know Philip! He said he'd be back in an hour—It's nearly that long now. I know Philip keeps his word."

"Here he comes!" cried Rose excitedly. "Hurry, Buddy, we're waiting for you!"

Philip was fairly running into the back yard.

"John was right," said Auntie. "He had faith in what Philip said. Faith in a person's word is very beautiful."

"And, when you're sick," said Rose, "Mother says it's a good thing to have faith in the doctor."

"And the medicine," said John.

"Horrid medicine!" Anna groaned, with a wiggle of disgust.

"Good medicine," corrected Rose, "if it makes you well. You know you were awfully sick, Anna Marie Madeleine, and the doctor's medicine made you well in one day."

"I was only a little sick," said Anna, closing her eyes. She did not like the way Rose shook her finger at her. Anna closed her eyes at everything that annoyed her.

"You were terribly sick!" cried Rose, really quite vexed.

"Hush!" said Auntie, "We're glad she's well again."

"But she never gives in, Auntie," complained Rose, her cheeks very red. "Anna says whatever she likes and never gives in when she's wrong."

"Anna," said Auntie very gravely, "is the littlest lamb of all."

"Big lambs," said Anna comfortably, "should be very good to the littlest ones," and she closed her eyes again, because Rose looked more than ready to contradict.

"And littlest ones," said Auntie, "should be very sweet and lovable. Sometimes little lambs, from too much petting, get spoiled. Then they are still the littlest, but not the easiest to love."

Anna sat up very straight, her eyes wide open and staring into Auntie's. "Oh, Auntie!" she cried. "Don't you love me?"

"Dearly," said Auntie, kissing the frightened-looking mouth. "Who said I didn't?"

"But—am I spoiled?"

"No, indeed," John hastily broke in; "you're the darlingest little sister that ever was!"

"But, Auntie," Anna said again, "am I spoiled?"

"So very slightly we can't really find out where," laughed Auntie.

"Oh dear!" sighed Anna. "And I never knew!"

Auntie folded her arms about the plump little form. "It's our fault, anyway, little one—we pet you too much."

"But I really like to be petted," whispered Anna.

"So does my little lamb over in the meadow," said Rose, good-natured again and sorry that she had teased Anna. "It loves me better than anybody else except its mother, because I pet it so much. It's little and cunning like you, Anna."

Anna was thinking hard. She paid small attention to what Rose was saying.

"I—," she swallowed excitedly and started again, "I mean not to be spoiled any more. I needn't be, even if I am the very littlest lamb of all!"

Anna's old friend, the bluebird, up in the elm tree gave the sweetest whistle just then! In fact, it was two whistles, and sounded exactly like a very sweet bird voice "Hurrah!"

"And," said Auntie, "I have faith in Anna's resolution. She has made up her mind, and our littlest lamb will surely not fail to do as she says."

"No, I shan't," said Anna, her eyes wide open.

"You have faith in Anna," said John, "and I had faith in Philip."

"And we have faith in our fathers and mothers," said Philip.

"And in Auntie," said Rose.

"But most of all," said Auntie, "we have faith in God. Fathers and mothers and aunties, and all the little lambs, have faith in God."

"No one could help believing what God says," said John.

"You see," said Auntie, "the more we love and respect people, the more ready we are to believe everything they say. We may not realize how much we trust certain people's word, but we are trusting all the time, nevertheless. Wouldn't it be a funny upside-down world if we believed only what we could see for ourselves, and understand without help? I knew a little girl who was a great trial to her teachers. Do you know why?"

"No, Auntie," said Anna.

"Was she so naughty?" asked Rose.

"She didn't intend to be naughty; she simply had no faith in anybody. And she was a very unhappy, dissatisfied child, besides annoying her teachers terribly. One day in her geography lesson, the teacher asked her, 'Where is Cape Horn?'—The little girl said, 'I don't know.' The teacher was almost too astonished to speak. At last she said, 'I told you less than a minute ago, dear, that it was at the southern end of South America. Have you forgotten so soon?' The little girl grew very red as she answered, 'I know what you told me, but I don't know whether Cape Horn is really there or not, because I never saw it.'"

All the children laughed.

"The story sounds like a joke, but it was a very unfortunate matter for that little girl. You understand that if people will believe only as much as they see, they must remain horribly ignorant. Luckily, most people are not like that foolish child; they practice faith every minute of their lives. Don't we all believe the mail will come, the car will start, airplanes have left Europe and are on the way to our city? We don't see everything we believe, even in the smallest affairs of our daily lives. Why, I haven't any idea what I shall have for lunch, although I believe firmly that it will presently be served. Little lambs, the whole world is run by faith, whether people stop to consider the fact or not. It is a faith in man, in his honesty, his strength, his justice. A liar is the most dangerous sort of a person, because he says things that can injure this faith among men which keeps the world going."

"We have to trust each other," said Philip.

"And we must tell the truth so people will know they can trust us," added Rose.

"Now God is Perfect Truth. He can neither deceive or be deceived. Are we going to be lacking in faith where He is concerned? We dare not. He is the Almighty One Who made us out of dust; more than that, He made the dust itself out of nothing."

"The dust out of nothing!" echoed Anna. "And the big sky with the shiny stars, and the pretty, darling moon—all out of nothing!"

"He made everything so beautiful," sighed John. And then, John's eyes grew very dark and very big. "He came upon earth Himself. That was the best of all, Auntie."

"Yes. He came on Christmas Day. Is it any wonder we have faith in Him? The Jews didn't have all the reasons for their faith which we have for ours. Above everything else, Jesus had not yet come. Don't you think we were very much favored by being born after our Good Shepherd had lived and died?"

"Yes indeed, Auntie."

"The Jews could not receive Him in Holy Communion. They knew God as a stern Father, not as the Good Shepherd. Their faith was great and blessed, but it could not be so happy and sweet as ours. God had not yet become man to dwell among His creatures. The Jews hadn't the faintest idea of what the tenderness and the gentleness of Jesus would be like."

"Still," said Philip, "they believed, Auntie."

"They had the precious gift of faith. Only God can give that gift. It is one of the three great virtues. Can you name them, Philip?"

"Faith, hope, and charity," answered Philip promptly.

"Faith must be the beginning," said John.

"Yes, because through faith we receive hope and charity. If we did not believe in God and all He teaches us, we couldn't hope in Him or love Him. The virtue of charity means the same as the virtue of love. Do the little lambs know when we receive the gift of faith?"

"I do!" cried Rose. "We receive the gift of faith in Baptism."

"That's right—The little baby receiving the mark of its Baptism is given faith."

"So we all have faith," said John.

"Of course," said Anna.

"It makes us believe in God and in all His teachings," said Auntie, "whether those teachings have been made known to us by God directly or through His Church."

"Mother says," said Rose, "the Church is like she is to us children—our mother. It tells us how to keep good, and friends with God, and what would hurt us, and where we mustn't go—like our other mother does."

"It takes care of us," said John.

"It takes care of us," Auntie repeated, "and it watches bravely and faithfully over that treasure it possesses, the Faith of Christ. It is the guardian of God's Truth. So we are very proud and happy to belong to the Church.

If we had to choose, we'd rather give up anything and everything else, rather than the Faith. You know the martyrs died rather than deny what faith taught them was true."

With a smile upon his lips, John sighed. He always envied the martyrs. Yet he knew that only a few of God's children could be martyrs. So he prayed a short, heartfelt prayer, which nobody else under the elm tree ever guessed at, that he might at least be as brave and true as a real martyr.

"I'm so tired!" murmured Anna.

"Never mind! You kept awake all through," said Auntie comfortingly. "To finish up, let's say what faith is, together. Ready?"

"Ready!" answered three children. Anna's head was nodding.

The bluebird heard Auntie and Rose, Philip, and John slowly repeat: "Faith is a divine virtue by which we believe in God and all He has taught.'"

Biblical Passages
1. Read Ephesians 2:19-22 on the Church.
2. On faith, read Hebrews 11:1.

Points of Doctrine
1. *What is the Church?* The Church is the congregation of all those who profess the faith of Christ, par-

take of the same sacraments, and are governed by their lawful pastors under one visible head.

2. *Why did Christ found the Church?* Christ founded the Church to teach, govern, sanctify, and save all men.

3. *How shall we know the things which we are to believe?* We shall know the things which we are to believe from the Catholic Church, through which God speaks to us.

4. *What is faith?* Faith is a divine virtue by which we firmly believe the truths which God has revealed.

Prayer to Memorize

Act of Faith
O Jesus, I believe in You.

Act of Faith

*O my God, I believe all the truths which
the Holy Catholic Church teaches,
because You have made them known. Amen.*

Act of Faith (longer form)

*O my God, I firmly believe that you are one God
in three divine Persons, Father, Son, and Holy Spirit.
I believe that your divine Son became man
and died for our sins and that he will come
to judge the living and the dead.
I believe these and all the truths
which the Holy Catholic Church teaches
because you have revealed them
who are eternal truth and wisdom,
who can neither deceive nor be deceived.
In this faith I intend to live and die. Amen.*

Hope

THERE are grown-up people who believe that little people have no troubles. But little people do have their troubles, and they hurt. Little people don't always talk about their sorrows; it would often be better if they did; because a wise grown-up can nearly always straighten out matters in a minute, while a small boy or girl may struggle on alone for a whole day or even longer.

To the four children under the elm tree, one of the griefs of childhood had come. Strictly speaking, it was more Rose's sorrow than anybody else's, because it was her pet lamb that had managed to stray from the flock and had been run over by a heavy plough. Still, whatever troubled one of the children disturbed the others, too. Rose and Anna were in tears, and Philip and John sniffled suspiciously when Auntie joined them for the morning talk.

"My darling lamb!" sobbed Rose. "Auntie, I can't think of anything else. The men say it will most surely d-d-die!"

"Not surely," consoled Auntie. "Don't give up, Rose dear. From all I hear, it has only one broken leg; I had a dog that was run over and had three broken legs, and still he lived. Don't cry so, dear child!"

It was no use. Rose put her head on the back of the seat and sobbed as though her heart would break.

"Oh, dear, oh, dear!" wailed Anna. "Auntie, if Rose's lamb dies, will you come to the funeral?"

"Hush!" said Philip with a choke. "It's not right to talk like that."

"We hope the lamb won't die," said John.

"Then there won't be any funeral," said Anna, "and what—what are we crying for?"

"Because," said Rose—indignantly raising her head, "my lamb is hurt and suffering and maybe going to die!"

"O-o-o-oh!" Anna began to weep at Rose's explanation of why they were, or had been, crying.

"Well," said Auntie, "I'm sorry to find four children so ready to despair. It's nice to love the dear little lamb so much, and to feel very sorry that it has been hurt; but do let's hope it will get well again. I myself really believe it will."

"Do you, Auntie?" asked Rose, turning her tear-stained face towards Auntie. "Do you really and truly believe my lamb will be all right again? And run to meet me? And crowd against me? And—and—" The memories were too much. Rose's eyes overflowed afresh, and she could not say another word.

Auntie drew Rose close beside her upon the bench. Anna squirmed a bit, jealous that one of Auntie's arms should be about Rose. But Auntie took no notice. Jealousy was one of Anna's small faults.

"Rose," said Auntie, "don't you know how to hope? You need to learn, if you want to be happy. Make up your mind, little girl, that all through your life you will hope until you are sure you can't reasonably hope any longer. Hope is a wonderful tonic. There are lots of times when it is a much better tonic than people can buy in a bottle and swallow from a spoon. I'm in earnest," as the children's tears changed to laughter. "Hope makes people strong, gives them courage. It prevents people from growing tired and giving up. A great deal of the bravery we hear of and read about owes its existence to hope. What sort of a soldier would a man make if he went into battle, hopeless of victory?"

"I suppose," said Philip, "to fight well, he must expect to win."

"Surely. He must feel 'As far as this battle depends upon me, it shall be a victory.' Take something that touches all of you little lambs: Would you study your lessons if you didn't hope to learn?"

"I never learn anything," said Anna, entirely undisturbed and no longer crying; "and I never study."

"That's why you don't learn," said Rose severely.

"Don't learn what?" asked Anna provokingly.

"You don't learn anything, because you don't study. You are very lazy, Anna Marie Madeleine, and everybody says so."

"I'm not!" cried Anna. "Nobody says so, 'cept you, Rose Mary Snow!"

"Speaking of hope," said Auntie very gravely, "I hope my little lambs are not going to argue. Arguing would be a frightful preparation for First Communion day. I hope we shall never have to mention the word again."

"Auntie has to hope, too," said Philip slyly.

"Of course I do. I have to hope ever so many things each day I live. If I hear it raining when I wake in the morning, I hope the sun will shine later, so we can have our meeting in the back yard. Then I hope all the little lambs are well, so they'll be able to come."

"And you hope we'll be good," suggested Rose.

"I hope you will learn something every single time we talk together. I prefer to take the goodness for granted."

"Sometimes we disappoint you," said Philip.

"Not often," Auntie declared. "I hope you won't ever be any worse than you are now. Of course, I hope you will even be much better, because the more you learn to love the Good Shepherd, the better lambs you will be, and it seems to me that no one could help loving Him more after He has come into the soul in Holy Communion. I hope that every Communion of your lives will make your souls stronger and more beautiful. See how often we hope, how we depend upon hope?"

"I hope we do," said Philip, and wondered why the others laughed. He had no idea that he seemed to be playing upon the word.

"We hope for good weather, for good health, for a good time generally," Auntie continued. "We hope to know our lessons, to please our fathers and mothers—"

"I hope," sighed Anna, "to keep awake."

"You needn't if you are too sleepy," said Auntie. "Now all these hopes we speak of so often and so thoughtlessly, are nothing compared with the divine virtue of hope. It is one of those three virtues relating so intimately to God and our own souls. We had faith yesterday, today we are considering hope, and tomorrow—" Auntie laughed, "I hope to tell you about charity. Hope, like the other two divine virtues, can be given us only by God. Can you tell me what hope is, John?"

"Hope is a divine virtue by which we hope for eternal life and everything necessary to obtain it, through Christ Jesus our Lord."

"Very good, John. Hope is our trust in God that through the sufferings of Jesus, our Good Shepherd, we shall reach heaven. Sometimes instead of heaven, we say 'everlasting life.' Our life here is only for a while, but in heaven, life will never end. Suppose we should have to be poor, or sick, or unhappy, or even all these at once; the poverty, sickness, and sadness would end when we died. Heaven will last forever. Therefore, the hope of the heaven that will never end will make us resigned to whatever God wills us to bear in this world. A moment ago we spoke of soldiers going into battle filled with the hope of earthly victory. We are soldiers, too, fighting for Jesus, our Good Shepherd, against His enemies. And the divine virtue of hope makes us brave to fight and steadfast to persevere. We know that with Jesus, we shall win. By the divine hope within us, we look forward to the reward at the end of the battle; knowing heaven is waiting for us, we struggle manfully through the fight with sin and Satan, each effort bringing us nearer the dear Lord we serve."

"We keep on because we hope in Him," said John.

"I'd like to be a soldier," said Philip.

"Even girls can be soldiers the way Auntie means," said Rose proudly.

"Let's all be soldiers of Jesus," said Auntie, "living on the divine virtue of hope, and fighting in the strength of that hope. Our banner is the sign of faith, the holy Cross. It is the sign of hope, too, because in that sign we hope to conquer all things upon the road to heaven. Finally, the holy Cross is the sign of charity as well, for our Good Shepherd died upon the Cross through love of us. Love the sign of the Cross, little lambs. Love it so that every glance you give it will be like an act of faith, hope and charity. There are people who always say, when they see a Cross, 'In this sign, we hope.' That is a beautiful practice—especially for soldiers of Jesus Christ. Through the divine virtue of hope, the tenderest, softest little lamb in the flock of the Good Shepherd may fight valiantly for Him."

"And with Him," said John, "in Holy Communion."

"Yes," said Auntie; "Jesus in Whom we hope, and because of Whom we hope, will be with us in the battle."

"And He will help us," said little Anna.

"Always," added Auntie, "those who hope in Jesus are never left alone. And He is with us in a very particular way by Holy Communion. Do you know what He said, so plainly that the words need not even be explained?"

"What, Auntie?" asked Rose.

"'Whoever eats my flesh, and drinks my blood remains in me and I in him.' That is why, little lambs, no matter how hard things may look, no matter how long the fight may last, you need never be conquered. Jesus, your hope, your Savior, your Good Shepherd, stays with you. With Him, in Him, and by Him, you may hope for everything necessary upon the way, and heaven at the end of your journey."

Rose gazed earnestly into Auntie's face.

"I can hope, because Jesus is so good, that He will cure my pet lamb?" she asked. "He cares about my lamb, doesn't He?"

"He cares about every single one of His creatures. The Bible tells us plainly that He cares for the birds of the air, and clothes the lilies of the field. Never be afraid to talk to Jesus about little things. He loves to have you tell Him about the slightest thing that interests you. He will be glad to listen to your prayer for the pet lamb."

"And I hope," said Rose fervently, "that the Good Shepherd will make it well again!"

There was no sign of tears as the little group broke up.

Biblical Passages
1. Read John 6:56.
2. Read Matthew 6:25-34.
3. Read 1 Corinthians 2:9 on the happiness of heaven.
4. On hope, read Psalm 39:8 and Sirach 2:10.

Points of Doctrine
1. *What is hope?* Hope is the divine virtue by which we firmly trust that God will give us eternal life and the means to obtain it.
2. *What is despair?* Despair is the loss of hope in God's mercy.
3. *What must we do to save our souls?* To save our souls we must worship God by faith, hope, and charity; that is, we must believe in Him, hope in Him, and love Him with all our heart.
4. *Does God see us?* God sees us and watches over us.
5. *Does God know all things?* God knows all things, even our most secret thoughts, words, and actions.

6. *Why are faith, hope, and love called virtues?* Faith, hope, and love are called virtues because they are not mere acts but habits by which we always and in all things believe God, hope in Him, and love Him.

7. *In what does the happiness of heaven consist?* The happiness of heaven consists in seeing the beauty of God, in knowing Him as He is, and in having every desire fully satisfied.

PRAYER TO MEMORIZE

Act of Hope

O Jesus, I hope in You.

Act of Hope

O my God, because You are all-powerful, merciful, and faithful to Your promises, I hope to be happy with You in heaven.

Act of Hope (longer form)

O Lord God,
I hope by your grace for the pardon of all my sins
and after life here to gain eternal happiness
because you have promised it,
who are infinitely powerful, faithful, kind,
and merciful.
In this hope I intend to live and die.
Amen.

CHARITY

JOHN was first at the old elm tree that morning. It was a beautiful June day, with the roses and honeysuckles in full bloom, and their sweet fresh perfume everywhere in the back yard.

"Such a pretty morning," John said to himself. He closed his eyes for a moment to hide the brightness, and then he suddenly opened them. "The yard seems to shine—and the sky shines—and the clouds"—John's eyes travelled delightedly over the snow-white, big puffy clouds moving across the blue. They looked like the sails of ships, blown out by the breeze—wonderful ships, where angels might hide, John thought. Some clouds seemed so low, one might imagine they dipped to touch the green hill opposite the yard. John smiled. "Even the sheep shine on the hill," his thoughts went on. "They look almost as pretty as the clouds. And they are nicer because they are alive."

John wondered, was it right to think the sheep nicer than the clouds?

Auntie came along and found him still trying to decide.

"Well, John," said Auntie, "all alone, aren't you?"

"Yes, so far, Auntie. I see the others coming though, Auntie." Hurriedly, because John was shy about asking questions when the other children were present, "Are the sheep really nicer than the clouds? I mean—it seems

67

to me that what is alive is more important than what is not alive."

"My dear, serious little John," said Auntie, "you think a great many things that are perfectly right."

"Oh!" said John, afraid Auntie was laughing at him.

"I'm not teasing, John. God has given us lots of earthly gifts which are precious, but the most precious of all is life. And although the sheep, being only animal, have no souls, they possess life and so come nearer to God's greatest earthly creature, man. Wait a minute, and we'll ask Philip what are the differences among God's creatures."

Auntie seated herself as Philip, Rose, and Anna came in sight.

"Clock was slow, clock was slow!" called Anna, hurrying to make sure of her place in Auntie's lap. "And we've been to see the lambs, too."

"Never mind!" Auntie said. "Don't trip and fall."

Plump, little Anna was quite out of breath as the group seated itself.

"What will the story be, Auntie?" asked Rose. "We've been guessing." Rose was very cheerful because her lamb was already a little better.

"Not too long," said Anna, quite as though she never lost a word by taking a nap. "Mother says I learn most from short stories."

"Because," said Philip, "you fall asleep so soon, you never hear more than the beginning."

"I don't," declared Anna.

"Instead of tormenting Anna," Auntie suggested, "suppose, Philip, you tell us what are the chief differences among God's living creatures."

The others giggled, and Philip looked mortified. Without his usual ease, he answered haltingly, "Angels have no bodies, being pure spirits, and men have bodies as well as souls."

"You forgot the third living creature, the lowest ones," Auntie hinted.

"Oh!" Philip was himself again. "Animals have bodies, but no souls," said he carelessly. Philip really did know a great deal.

"And our life," said John, "was breathed into us by God."

"That's why we are so very far above the animals," Auntie explained. "In the Bible, we read how God made us but a 'little less than the angels'—only a little lower than those pure spirits who see God always face-to-face."

"Angels never do wrong," said Rose.

"They obey God always," added John.

"And Holy Communion," said Auntie, "is often called 'The Bread of Angels'—the food fit for angels, the food that will make us pure and good like the angels."

"And help us to do God's Will, the way they do," said John.

"Because we love God like they do," Rose said.

"Love, or charity, is our story today," said Auntie. "Love is what makes the Lord Jesus call Himself our Good Shepherd, love made Him come upon earth, love made Him give us Holy Communion. We want to receive Him, then, when He comes to us, with all the love our hearts will hold."

"Our hearts will hold," Anna repeated. "Are our hearts very little, Auntie?"

"They need not be. At least, if we fill them with love, everything small and mean will be crowded out."

Anna slipped down from Auntie's lap, darted behind the old elm, and stooping, scooped up a handful of soft earth from between the roots of the tree.

"Anna's hand is full of earth," Anna laughed mischievously. "Nothing else can get in!"

"That's what I mean. And, children, we want to be particularly careful not to let our hearts be *full of earth*."

"You mean, Auntie," said John, "not clay like Anna has scooped up, but all the things in this world, don't you?"

"I do. God has given us so many beautiful things, to show more and more His love for us, but we must remember Who gave us all we have, and for everything we enjoy we must love Him more. Then our hearts won't be filled with earth, but filled with love, the more we have of earth's joy and beauty."

"God made the flowers," said Anna, casting the clay aside and reaching for a daisy. She climbed back into Auntie's lap and fastened the daisy in Auntie's hair.

"Love Him for the flowers," said Auntie softly.

"He made the sheep and the little lambs," said Rose.

"Love Him for those."

"He made the sky and the ocean and the mountains," said Philip.

"And He made us, to go to heaven," said John.

"He made the whole beautiful world," said Auntie. "He made this lovely day, He sends us the light and the breeze and health to enjoy His gifts. His love is all around us, like the sea is around a tiny speck floating upon its surface."

"I've seen the sea," said Philip. "It seems never to end."

"God never does end," said John.

"The sea is about the nearest idea we can really grasp of the greatness of God's love," said Auntie. "It is so big, and so strong, and every river in the world at last flows into it. Even the sea, though, can be measured, and God's love cannot. But while we are here, in this world, with our minds able to understand only a wee bit of all there is to learn, the sea is a help in thinking about the great, wide love of God."

"Does He love each one all for Himself?" Rose asked.

"Each and every one, down to the tiniest baby in all the world. For any one of us, all alone, our Good Shepherd would have given His life."

The children looked silently and earnestly at Auntie.

"Jesus would die just for me, all alone?" asked John after a while.

"Just for you, John, all alone, because He loves you so much. In return for so much love, wouldn't it be a shame not to love Him at least as much as we could?"

"Yes," said John, very seriously. "Auntie, it would be an awful shame."

"I do love God," said Anna decidedly. "I love Him very much." She stretched out her short plump arms. "I love Him as big as the ocean!"

"Jesus stretched out His arms on the Cross," said Philip. "Mother said that was to show us how He died with arms open for all the world."

"No one would He leave out," said Auntie. "Jesus wants us every single one. Now, sure that we do love Him, what else must we do, in order to be filled with the love, or charity, that is so dear to God?"

"I know," said Rose eagerly. "We must love our neighbor."

"Neighbor," said Anna. "That's the people in the next house."

"Sometimes," smiled Auntie, "God does not mean only the people in the next house, though; to love our neighbor, children, means to love every human being."

"Oh, Auntie," said John, "we couldn't!"

"Some are horrid," said Rose.

Auntie laid her fingers softly on Rose's mouth.

"Some are awfully dirty," said Philip. Philip's collar was always clean, and his shoelaces were never untied.

Auntie shook her head at Philip.

"We can't love all people alike," said Auntie. "But we can love them all as much as God expects us to love them, if we try. Charity, or the virtue of love, forbids us saying anyone is horrid"—Rose blushed brightly—"It would also check us when we felt like criticizing. If some people are awfully dirty"—Philip dropped his eyes—"probably no one ever taught them to be neat. Suppose nobody had ever taught us? We ought to be neat—very, very neat, especially because we are allowed to receive our Good Shepherd in Holy Communion—but we have been carefully taught. Would our Good Shepherd, so gentle and so tender, blame little lambs who were dirty because they knew no better?"

"He never would," said Anna very solemnly.

"The way to love everybody is to remember Jesus loves us all," Auntie went on. "We want to be like Jesus, we want to do as He wishes. Dare we dislike anyone for whom Jesus died? We see the faults of other people, and they see ours. The virtue of charity makes us over-look the faults of others and try to correct our own."

"It turns things around," said Philip.

"That's a fine way to explain what charity does," said Auntie. "It makes us hard upon ourselves, and easy and generous with others. Remember it is a divine virtue—divine means coming from God, you remember. We receive it from our Father in heaven."

"Sometimes you say 'charity,' Auntie, and sometimes you say 'love,'" said John. "Do they mean the same?"

"Yes, John. The virtue of charity and the virtue of love are the same."

"But Auntie," said Rose, "I thought charity meant giving things to poor people?"

"Giving to the poor is exercising charity; for love of God, you love His creatures, and because you love them you are glad to help them—happy to give to them. Hearts full of love can't possibly be selfish. Love longs to give, love forgets itself. See how far our Good Shepherd's love for us has carried Him: it makes Him, our Lord and Savior, so generous that He gives us Himself —His whole, perfect, living Self—in Holy Communion."

"He couldn't do any more," said John softly.

"No, the love of God could do no more. You are getting ready for Holy Communion. There are many things for which we prepare in this world. They need different preparations. For a party, we want our prettiest clothes."

"And for rain, we want umbrellas," said Philip.

"Quite true. For a journey, we take tickets and luggage. For school, we need books. It's only a very stupid person who makes the wrong preparation. Now above all—we mustn't be stupid about holy things. Our Good Shepherd is the God of Wisdom; we can and ought to ask Him to make us bright and clever in our service of Him. Can you guess how we may safely judge our cleverness?"

Four pairs of eager eyes gazed expectantly at Auntie, but no one spoke.

"The way to measure our cleverness in the service of our Good Shepherd," Auntie went on after a pause, "is to find out how much we love Him. Love is the most important part of the preparation for Holy Communion. It is by far the best portion of the welcome we ought to give Jesus. Love will make Him forgive everything else that may be lacking. You might put your souls in order, but leave them cold, because no love was in them. Suppose you cleaned and polished everything in a room; then you shut out every bit of light and heat. How would a guest feel, placed in such a room?"

"He would not like it at all," said Anna. "I hate the dark, and I hate to be cold."

"A soul without love for the Good Shepherd Who visits it, is like a cold, dark room. It may be clean and in order, but there is no sunshine to light it and to make it warm. Love for Jesus is the light, the joy, the glory of the soul; love for Jesus makes the proper welcome for Him in Holy Communion. It rests with us to receive Him with as much love as our hearts will hold. Little lambs, going to receive Holy Communion for the first time, think a great deal about the virtue of love. Pray that God will give you largely of this divine virtue, which is so fitting for lambs of the Good Shepherd. Then, when Jesus comes to you, you will be able to say, 'I am very little and I don't know much, but I am so glad to receive you, Lord Jesus, because I love you!'"

To Auntie's surprise, the four children clasped their hands as though told to do so, and said together, "I am so glad to receive you, Lord Jesus, because I love you."

Biblical Passages
1. Read Psalm 8:5-6.
2. Read 1 Corinthians 13:13.
3. Read John 3:16.

Points of Doctrine
1. *What is charity?* Charity is the divine virtue by which we love God above all things for His own sake, and our neighbor as ourselves for the love of God.
2. *What are the commandments that contain the whole law of God?* The commandments that contain the whole law of God are these two: 1) You shall love the Lord your God with your whole heart, with your whole soul, and with your whole strength, and with your whole mind; and 2) You shall love your neighbor as yourself.
3. *Is it well to receive Holy Communion often?* It is well to receive Holy Communion often, as nothing is a greater aid to a holy life than often to receive the Author of all grace and the Source of all good.
4. *What should we do after Holy Communion?* After Holy Communion, we should spend some time in adoring our Lord, in thanking Him for the grace we have received, and in asking Him for the blessings we need.

Prayer to Memorize

Act of Love

O Jesus, I love You with all my heart.

Act of Love

O my God, because You are all-good,
I love You with my whole heart and soul.
Amen.

Act of Love (longer form)

O Lord God, I love you above all things
and I love my neighbor for your sake
because you are the highest, infinite and perfect
good, worthy of all my love.
In this love I intend to live and die.
Amen.

The House of God

WHEN Auntie and the children gathered under the old elm tree, Auntie was looking very serious. It was Monday morning, and the day before Auntie and the children had seen an usher take two small boys out of church.

"You know there was some trouble among the boys yesterday," began Auntie, "and that during the homily, two were taken out."

Philip and Rose burst out laughing.

"They were awfully red," said Anna. "I don't wonder. I don't want any big man to tell me to leave the church!"

"Nobody ever will," said John.

"You know how to behave," said Auntie. "Those boys had been nudging and tickling each other from the beginning of Mass. And when one of them took a white mouse out of his pocket as the homily began—" Auntie waited.

"The white mouse may have seemed funny," she said when the children had grown quiet. "Only, did it ever strike you that church was the proper place in which to be funny?"

Rose and Philip looked uncomfortable. John wondered whether he might have laughed, too, had he seen the white mouse, and Anna nodded her head in comical approval of Auntie's gravity.

"It is cheap to be funny," said Auntie. "It is also perfectly proper, in a fitting place. White mice are cunning little things, in the eyes of most boys at least; only in church is not where we play with pet animals. Those boys had no intention of simply playing with the mouse anyway. They wanted to laugh and make other people laugh." Rose choked over another giggle. "Laugh it out, Rose," said Auntie. "You see a back yard is a jolly place for laughing. The yard is not church."

Now just as soon as Rose was told to laugh as much as she liked, she no longer wanted to laugh at all! Very often we are that way: Something seems perfectly delicious to us as long as it is forbidden, and as soon as it is allowed us, we don't want it a bit. That is because our human nature left to itself is always inclined to disobey. The help from God, which we call His grace, is the only power that can make us love to obey.

"To be merry and happy," Auntie went on, "is right. To be happy in church is particularly right and fitting, for our Good Shepherd is there and we can't help being glad in His Presence. But our Good Shepherd is the great God, the King of Kings, the Creator of everything. We are very small and helpless; we owe everything to Him. In His House we must be respectful as well as loving. Even in your everyday lives, you don't treat all persons alike, do you?"

"No, Auntie," Rose answered. "We don't treat Mommy like we treat each other."

"Surely not. You love your mother better than your small friends, yet you wouldn't tease and romp with your mother the way you do with each other."

"No, indeed," said Anna. "Mommy is Mommy."

78

Anna was very little and had her own way of saying things; but Auntie knew exactly what Anna meant. Mother and Father were above and apart from other people in the world of the children. Mothers and fathers must receive a respect all their own.

"If the president invited you to visit him in Washington, you would show still another respect for him while you were his guests," said Auntie.

"And we have to be awfully respectful to grandfathers and grandmothers," said Philip, "because they are so much older."

"Even Father and Mother have to," said Rose; "because they are only Grandfather's and Grandmother's children."

"Such big children!" laughed Anna, who thought all grown people were about a thousand years old.

"And Grandfather and Grandmother, and Father and Mother, like all of us, are God's children," said Auntie. "You see there is no word big enough to express how much respect we owe God. In church, we are in His House—His guests."

"It's more than if the president invited us," said Philip.

"It is so much more that we can't realize how great the honor really is. Our president and the kings of other countries are served by men. In church the angels wait, adoring God day and night. If with our bodily eyes, we could see the angels before the altar, how ashamed of ourselves we should be!" Rose shifted in her seat.

"I didn't think, when I laughed at the white mouse," she said.

"Most of the things we do that are not right, are done because we don't think," said Auntie. "Don't look so distressed, Rose. These talks are not meant to make anyone unhappy; they are simply to help us all to know our Good Shepherd better, and knowing Him better, to serve Him more truly."

"It is easy to serve Him by being quiet in church," said John.

"Not always," smiled Auntie. "For instance, when somebody lets loose a white mouse, it's rather hard not to laugh."

"Oh!" said Rose eagerly. "Then it wasn't so awful to laugh, was it?"

"No, it was very natural, and almost excusable. The real fault lies with the lad who tried to distract people."

"Perhaps," said John, "he did not think, either."

"That's a very good way to judge him. But as for us, we intend to think about how we act in the House of God, don't we?"

"Yes, Auntie," came the answer.

"We mean to remember that Jesus lives in the church. Before we take our places, we shall genuflect carefully, saying a word of love to Jesus as we bend our knee."

"What should we say, Auntie?" asked Philip.

"Anything that comes from your heart. Perhaps 'I adore Thee, Jesus,' or 'Jesus, I love Thee,' or maybe just 'My Jesus.' The one thing we must do is realize that we are bending our knee to God—to Jesus in the Blessed Sacrament. If you came into a room where I was, you would look at me when you greeted me, wouldn't you?"

"Certainly, Auntie."

"You would call me by name—recognize me. Now never neglect to recognize Jesus when you genuflect. Look towards the tabernacle, and greet the Good Shepherd. 'I know mine, and mine know me,' Jesus said. Show that you do know Him when you enter His House, the church. You would never say, 'Good morning, Auntie,' turning your back upon me and looking out of the window. Don't be less respectful to our Blessed Lord than you are to a human being."

"If we just think Jesus is very near," said John, "we'll be all right."

"Exactly. In church, you are as near to Him as the people used to crowd when He lived in Galilee. You don't need to be grown-up to understand that in the church you are visiting Jesus in His own Home. And, little lambs, form the habit of paying attention to the Good Shepherd while you are before Him in the Blessed Sacrament. Lots of grown people fidget and fuss in church because while they were children they never formed the habit of being quiet and respectful. You are so little, you could form almost any habit."

"Yes," sighed Rose, "and we mostly form bad ones!"

"Oh, I think not," laughed Auntie. "Anyway, this one of behaving properly in church is bound to be a good habit."

"Must we sit still without moving?" asked Anna in alarm.

"No, indeed. Do you think the Good Shepherd would be cruel to His little lambs? Just remember where you are. Think that you are joining the angels in adoring Jesus in the Blessed Sacrament. Talk to the Good Shepherd—tell Him anything, everything. Tell Him, if you like, that you know laughing and playing are very good in their places, but church is the place for other things; and as for you, you want the Good Shepherd to teach you those things. You mean to think of Him in a special way while you are in His House. You don't wish to prevent others from thinking of Him by talking or being silly, like the boy who took the white mouse to church in his pocket."

"He was silly," said Rose thoughtfully.

"A clown is all right in the circus," said Auntie. "The clown may be a saint; but if he is a saint, he surely won't act like a clown in church. Jesus found people buying and selling in the temple at Jerusalem one day; He cast them out, telling them that His House was a House of Prayer. There is a splendid lesson for us, coming directly from the Good Shepherd Himself. Buying and selling are perfectly good in themselves; they are only not fit for church."

"Because it is God's House," said Rose.

"And we must pay 'tention to Jesus there," added Anna.

"Yes; the little lambs go to church to visit their Good Shepherd. And while they are with Him, they want to give Him all their thoughts. They need not repeat long prayers, but they need to remember Whose guests they are, and to behave as though they remembered."

"Yes," said Anna, very gravely, "I think so, too!"

And the bigger children agreed with her.

Biblical Passages
1. Read Mark 11:15-17.
2. Regarding behavior in church, read 1 Timothy 3:15.

Points of Doctrine

1. *What is the Mass?* The Mass is the unbloody sacrifice of the Body and Blood of Christ.
2. *What is a sacrifice?* A sacrifice is the offering of an object by a priest to God alone, and the consuming of it to acknowledge that He is the Creator and Lord of all things.
3. *Is the Mass the same sacrifice as that of the Cross?* The Mass is the same sacrifice as that of the Cross.
4. *How should we assist at Mass?* We should assist at Mass with great interior recollection and piety and with every outward mark of respect and devotion.
5. *Which is the best manner of hearing Mass?* The best manner of hearing Mass is to offer it to God with the priest for the same purpose for which it is said, to meditate on Christ's sufferings and death, and to go to Holy Communion.

Prayers to Memorize

Prayer when Blessing with Holy Water

By this holy water and Your Precious Blood,
Wash away all my sins, O Lord.

Or:

Fatima Pardon Prayer

My God, I believe, I adore, I trust and I love You!
I beg pardon for all those that do not believe,
do not adore, do not trust,
and do not love You.
Amen.

Or:

Fatima Angel's Prayer of Adoration

*Oh Most Holy Trinity, Father, Son and Holy Spirit,
I adore You profoundly.
I offer You the most precious Body, Blood,
Soul, and Divinity of Jesus Christ
present in all the tabernacles of the world,
in reparation for the outrages, sacrileges,
and indifferences by which He is offended.
By the infinite merits of the Sacred Heart of Jesus
and the Immaculate Heart of Mary,
I beg the conversion of poor sinners.
Amen.*

The Fair White Page

S UPPOSE," began Auntie, taking Anna upon her knee, "each one of you could obtain any possible wish, which would it be?"

Auntie did not usually start with a question. The children were surprised and did not answer at once. As the silence became marked, Philip, feeling the responsibility of being "the oldest," spoke first. "I'd wish to be a man like Father," said he.

Here was a fine clue, and Rose took advantage of it.

"I'd wish to grow up and be like Mother," then said she, beaming at the pleasant ambition.

"What would you wish?" John asked Anna.

Anna looked at John, at Auntie, at the rustling trees. She even looked at the sheep over on the hillside. The world was very lovely.

"I don't know," sighed Anna at last; "I believe I don't wish anything."

"Yes, you do wish something," declared John, and he whispered something in the small sister's ear.

"Oh, I know!" cried Anna, clapping her chubby hands. "John says I'd wish to go to heaven!"

Rose was a trifle mortified that she had not thought of that wish herself. But Auntie said, "We all wish that, darling; it's a general wish. I mean, which particular wish would you make?"

Anna stared doubtfully.

"I'm not parlic'lar," said she, and closed her eyes when the others laughed.

"Anna is contented, at least," said Auntie. "John, you haven't told us what your own wish would be?"

John flushed. "I'd like to love the Good Shepherd," said he.

"That is a beautiful wish," said Auntie. "And now, what do you think I'd wish?"

The little lambs were at a loss. What could Auntie wish? She was grown up, and had been graduated, she was taller than their mothers, she surely loved the Good Shepherd—of course she was going to heaven some day. What could Auntie possibly wish?

"Sometimes," said Auntie, "I wish it so much that I feel actually homesick."

Auntie's lips were twitching, and yet they knew she was in earnest.

"But you are home," said Rose.

"She's going visiting after First Communion," said Philip, not happy at the thought.

"Never mind, she's here now," said Rose firmly. Rose preferred not to think of unpleasant things.

"I'm here now, and I'm wishing something," Auntie persisted, growing very serious.

Anna's lip suddenly trembled. She wouldn't have Auntie deprived of anything.

"Oh, Auntie, can't you get it?" cried the child, very greatly distressed.

"No, I can't get the wish," Auntie answered.

Tears seemed so near that Auntie hurried to say, "My wish would be to be as little as the littlest of you!"

"O-o-oh!" breathed Anna, her eyes very big indeed. "Auntie, you wouldn't wish to be like me?"

86

"Yes," said Auntie; "I'd love to be as little as you!"

"But why?" asked Rose in astonishment.

"It's awful not to know anything," said Philip, thinking in disgust of his arithmetic. "I wish people could be born grown up and educated."

"I don't," said Rose decidedly; "we shouldn't have baby brother."

"And John wouldn't have me," said Anna indignantly.

"Jesus came as a little Baby," said John, smiling at his sister.

"And Jesus loves childhood," said Auntie. "I'm glad I didn't have to be born grown up, Philip, although I've had to study hard in order to learn something. I'd rather, you see, go back and be a little child again, if only I could!"

To the children, this seemed very odd indeed.

"Why, Auntie?" asked John. He was wondering whether he, after years and years had passed, would ever wish he could be a stupid little boy again, trying very hard to grow less stupid as the bright days went by.

"Why?" Auntie repeated after John. "I'd like to be one of you, because your lives are all ahead of you, and just imagine how much you can make of them! Perhaps, if I could have a second chance, I'd do better with mine," and lively, grown-up Auntie, who was so big, and knew so much, sighed the way little Anna sometimes sighed!

"You couldn't be any better," Anna solemnly declared.

"That's lovely," laughed Auntie. "Anyway, in childhood the soul is like a fair white page, and you may write upon it whatever you choose."

Rose looked anxious. "Maybe," said she, "the page is not all white."

"We're not always good, you know," Philip said. He was very honest.

"Perhaps it is a wee bit blotted or scratched, that fair white page," Auntie admitted. "But there is the Precious Blood to make it perfectly fair again in the Sacrament of Penance. And Jesus is coming to give it a beauty something like the beauty of the angels in heaven. So you are starting at seven or eight, with the Good Shepherd Himself, to help you live your lives for Him."

"Our souls are surely white at Holy Communion," said John.

"As white as snow. And the little lambs making their First Communion ought to very earnestly ask the Good Shepherd to keep them white. Tell Him you know what a blessing it is to have Him come into your souls so soon. Tell Him you understand that His coming is the greatest help to write only beautiful things on the fair white page of your innocence. Everybody's life is like a story told to God. He never misses a single word. Ask the Good Shepherd to show you how to have your lives the sort of story God loves."

"But we'll make mistakes, won't we?" asked Rose.

"Yes, you will make mistakes. God will not be angry if they are only mistakes. He will help you rub them out and fill in the things which should have taken their places. And if a real sin should come upon the soul, like an ugly blot upon the fair white page, you must be very sorry, but never give up. The Precious Blood will wash the spot away, and you may start again."

"With the fair white page," said John dreamily.

"Sometimes only a very small fault, like a wee bit of dust, may dull the page. Then you need not receive the Sacrament of Penance in order to be forgiven. If you say an Act of Love, or an Act of Contrition, the love and sorrow in your heart will brighten the page once more."

"And you said, Auntie," said John, "that we could write beautiful things on the page of our souls?"

"Yes. We don't want the fair white page simply a blank, do we? If you sent your father the most beautiful sheet of paper in the world, carefully placed in a sealed envelope, what would your father say?"

"He would laugh," said Philip.

"He'd be disappointed," said Rose.

"He certainly would wish there had been a letter, and not a blank sheet," said Auntie. "If you only keep out of sin, the page of your soul is beautiful, but it is blank. You want to write upon the page: Tiny little acts done for God—kind words said to one another— your homework done without complaint—some errands done for an older person—a favor for a little friend. Oh, there are dozens of things possible for the littlest lambs which will fill the fair white page of First Communion day with the golden story of a beautiful life!"

"You mean beautiful to God," said John.

"Yes, I mean beautiful to God. For His sake, for the sake of our Good Shepherd, we will avoid everything ugly, everything that would spoil the white page, and besides we will fill it with lovely things. Do you know that the smallest thing done for Jesus, is something beautiful upon the page?"

"Really, Auntie?" asked Rose. "Even taking good care of my pet lamb?" Rose's eyes were shining. She would like to think that the small duties of her day were really and truly able to beautify the white page that would be hers at First Communion.

"Surely. The act itself is small, yet done for Jesus it grows great and beautiful. He Himself has told us that a cup of cold water given in His Name will be rewarded. A cup of cold water is nearly nothing, yet God remembers it. He is too great to forget even the smallest of our actions. The Good Shepherd will be pleased each time Rose Mary Snow does anything for Him—and He will not leave out the times she cares for her pet lamb."

"That's lovely, Auntie," sighed Rose.

Anna's forehead was puckered almost into a knot, and she was very still.

"What is it, Anna darling?" asked Auntie.

"Oh, never mind!" murmured Anna.

"But of what are you thinking?"

Anna's forehead straightened out.

"I was thinking," said Anna. She had not answered Auntie's question.

"We know that, dear. Tell us what wrinkled your face so?"

"Oh, well—I don't think I like to look for Grandmother's glasses when she loses them 'most every minute." Anna was solemn as an owl.

"And so—" Auntie prompted.

"I wanted something to put on my own white page," said Anna, speaking fast but with dignity; "and I'm going to look for the glasses every single time, while Grandmother is visiting us."

Auntie gathered the plump little creature in her arms.

"That is simply splendid!" said Auntie. "I am sure every little lamb here is going to start as well as Anna. Then if you keep on, when you are grown-up men and women and look back at First Communion day, you will be able to think, 'The Good Shepherd came to me at the beginning of my life as a reasonable being; and thanks to the tender love for His little lambs, which made Him come, I have not spoiled the fair white page He gave me for my own.'"

The sunshine of the yard was around the Good Shepherd's little lambs, like His love surrounding their souls. There were no clouds in the bright blue sky; there were no serious sins upon the consciences of the children. Clouds, when they came, would darken the sun; sin, if it won, would stain the whiteness of the souls that day still so near the purity of the angels. When Auntie parted from the children, behind her smiles and kisses there was an earnest prayer that Rose and John, Anna, and Phillip might never disfigure, by grievous sin, the fair white pages that would be theirs upon First Communion day.

Biblical Passages
1. On being little, read Matthew 18:1-5 and 19:14.
2. Read too Matthew 10:40-42 and Matthew 25:31-46.

Points of Doctrine
1. *Why should we be sorry for our sins?* We should be sorry for our sins, because sin is the greatest of evils and an offence against God our Creator, Preserver, and Redeemer, and because it shuts us out of heaven and condemns us to the eternal pains of hell.

2. *How many kinds of contrition are there?* There are two kinds of contrition: perfect contrition and imperfect contrition.
3. *What is perfect contrition?* Perfect contrition is that which fills us with sorrow and hatred for sin, because it offends God, who is infinitely good in Himself and worthy of all love.
4. *What is imperfect contrition?* Imperfect contrition is that by which we hate what offends God, because by it we lose heaven and deserve hell; or because sin is so hateful in itself.
5. *Is imperfect contrition sufficient for a worthy confession?* Imperfect contrition is sufficient for a worthy confession, but we should endeavor to have perfect contrition.

Prayer of Service

Prayer of St. Ignatius Loyola

Dearest Lord, teach me to be generous.
Teach me to serve you as you deserve;
to give and not to count the cost;
to fight and not to heed the wounds;
to labor and not to seek to rest;
to give of myself and not to ask for reward,
except the reward of knowing
that I am doing your will. Amen.

Service of God

FOUR very sweet faces awaited Auntie. Wee Anna was quiet and thoughtful, and sat with clasped hands. As Auntie came into the back yard, the children rose to go meet her, but their welcome, if more affectionate than ever before, was decidedly less noisy.

"Good morning, good children of the Good Shepherd!" cried Auntie. "Dear lambs of His true fold, I ought to say! I see happiness all around, while I don't hear so much of it as usual."

"When you're awfully glad," said Philip, "you get quiet."

"And remember things," said Rose.

"And you laugh inside instead of out loud," John explained.

"I don't laugh at all, Buddy," declared Anna. "I'm just glad First Communion is coming."

"Not for you, Anna," said Rose.

"Yes, it is," replied Anna gravely, "I'm going the very next time."

"You certainly are," said Auntie. "As I came along this morning, I was thinking over what we'd talk about. Won't it be a fine idea to settle firmly in our minds to Whose service we intend promising ourselves? We are in it now, but we are going to realize it better, strengthen ourselves to be more faithful. Whose service is it?"

"God's," said Philip.

"God's," echoed the other three.

"Our answer is ready." said Auntie; "We know we wish to be upon God's side. The Good Shepherd's little lambs mean to stay always in His care, forever within His fold. Almost without a thought, they would answer anyone who asked them whom they wanted to serve, that they belonged to Jesus the Good Shepherd and of course would serve Him."

"Sometimes people call Jesus 'the Master,'" Philip remarked.

"Very often. Our Good Shepherd is, in fact, the Master of all men. The trouble is that everybody is not faithful to this Master. You see, He does not make us serve Him, He never forces us. We are free to choose."

"Choose what?" asked Anna, whose attention had wandered.

"Free to choose our Master," Auntie answered. "We ought to choose Jesus, our Good Shepherd. And we do, don't we?"

"Oh, yes, Auntie," came a hearty answer.

"We won't choose sin; we won't work for Satan, will we?"

"No indeed, Auntie," as heartily as before.

"At Holy Communion, we can promise Jesus to try all our lives to be His true servants. Above all, we should promise Him at First Communion that we will never forget what we owe Him for coming to us. Our First Communion day shall be the brightest and the clearest memory of our lives, no matter how very old we may live to be. Jesus comes to us; He is holy, beautiful. He is God. Nobody, not even the Blessed Mother, can be compared with His holiness and His beauty, because no creature can rightly be compared with God. Think a minute, little lambs: Jesus is God."

Anna closed her eyes. "Jesus is God," she repeated.

"And God is the Good Shepherd," added John.

"And we are His own little lambs!" Anna went on, her voice very serious indeed.

"Great as He is," said Auntie, "He wants our service. We are not too little for Him. Suppose we took a long, tiresome journey across mountains and seas and at last stopped at the palace of a rich and powerful king. We might wait a long time before the king had time to see us. But let's imagine he did see us, after we waited a while. We'd make Philip speak for us, something like this: 'Mighty King, we heard about Your Majesty in a country thousands of miles away. We have travelled far, and now we ask to be taken into Your Majesty's household.' What do you suppose the king would say?"

Rose and Philip laughed.

"He'd say we were very silly," said Philip.

"That he didn't need us," said John hastily. "A king would be polite, wouldn't he, Auntie?"

"Yes. He would be very polite, but very certain that there were plenty of people already in his household, and he could not turn them out for strangers. Our weary travels would be for nothing. We should find that the great king had never before heard of us, and would never miss us after we left him."

"His people, though, would be proud that they belonged to his household," said John.

"Of course. I hope they wouldn't let us see them laugh at us for our foolish running after earthly honor, but perhaps after we had gone, they'd laugh good and hard."

95

"I'm not going to that king," said Anna decidedly. "I'm going to Jesus."

"We are going to Jesus, our Good Shepherd. He is King of Kings, and Master of the world. He made even the greatest and best king that ever lived, out of dust. He rules the earth and the heavens. But He wants our service, because although He is so mighty and wise, and we are so weak and dull, He loves us. Children, sometimes it seems more wonderful that people can offend God, than that the martyrs died for Him."

"Why, Auntie?" asked Rose.

"God is so good, He watches us so tenderly, He helps us so much, dear, isn't it strange we can disobey Him? How can anyone created by God, and saved by God's love from the punishment sin deserves, find it in his heart to insult the Heavenly Father, the Good Shepherd?"

"It's awful," said Philip.

"Sin is awful. It must surprise the angels. You know the angels serve God faithfully always. The martyrs can't surprise the angels; the angels, too, would be true to death. The martyrs appreciate God's gifts. They die cheerfully, with a smile, when the service of God can be done no other way. It's not only our duty to serve God; it is our greatest privilege. We are allowed to serve the Almighty God; we are permitted to do His Holy Will. Oh, dare we refuse?"

"No, no, Auntie," said Rose earnestly.

"The devils were once angels," said Auntie. "They lived in heaven with God. And we know why they were put out of heaven. They said to God, 'We will not serve.' It would be terrible, wouldn't it, to take sides with those unhappy beings who were once in heaven and are now in hell? The Good Shepherd's little lambs are meant for heaven. He is coming to them in order to make it easy and sweet to serve Him so that they may live forever in His beautiful home. If there is pleasure in serving those we love, if we are proud to serve anyone important in the eyes of men—"

"Like the president?" asked Philip.

"Yes, or some brave general back from a war, or a good and just king, or a famous inventor, or anybody who is respected by the world—how much happier, how much prouder, may we be to serve Jesus Christ?"

The breeze sighed softly in the trees, as Auntie stopped speaking. Then John sighed softly, too. John wished he could be sure of serving the Good Shepherd in the very best way, all his life. The Good Shepherd heard that wish, although John said nothing, because all our thoughts are known to God. Jesus not only knows every single thought of His creatures; He remembers, too. And in His loving tenderness He must have blessed little John for the wish which came from the bottom of the boy's heart.

"After First Communion," said Rose, "we promise to renounce Satan and give ourselves to Jesus Christ forever."

"Yes. After First Communion, you kneel at the altar and make the promises yourselves; they are the same promises that others made for you when you were baptized. You make the choice; you say plainly whom you will serve. Satan will have nothing of you. He is the Evil One, and you put him down. You will not obey him; you belong to the Master, Jesus Christ. Satan's lies will not tempt you. Satan's servants end in hell. The servants of Jesus Christ, the lambs of the Good Shepherd, travel through this world to heaven."

"It will be lovely in heaven," said Anna. "I have two baby brothers there. They see Jesus all the time."

"And so shall we," said Auntie. "Heaven will be our reward for the service of God. Think of the unfortunate people who listen to Satan, serve him, and then have to spend forever with him in hell! What a sad mistake they made, when they took their choice! Satan deceives, and afterwards gathers in the miserable ones who believed his lies. Little lambs, let us thank our Good Shepherd that He has us under His care; let us promise Him with our whole hearts to stay in His happy service; if we even begin to wander toward the edge of the fold, when our conscience warns us like the sheepdog yonder barks at the wayward lambs, let's run back to the dear Shepherd at once."

"We will," said the children solemnly.

"If Rose's lamb had stayed in the meadow," said Anna, "it wouldn't have been run over."

"Surely not. And if we stay close to our Good Shepherd, Who comes into our hearts at Holy Communion, we shall not be hurt by sin. Before we end our talk this morning, children, don't you want to repeat the promises you will make after Holy Communion?"

Down upon their knees they went. Auntie had not meant them to kneel, but when four pairs of hands were clasped and four heads bent, she did not tell the little lambs to rise. Instead, Auntie knelt, too; and the birds heard—but much more, the Good Shepherd and His angels heard—very loving voices say, "'I renounce Satan, with all his works and pomps, and give myself to Jesus Christ forever.'"

Biblical Passages
1. Read the comforting verses of Psalm 139:1-12.
2. Read 1 Corinthians 10:13 on temptation.

Points of Doctrine
1. *Did all the angels God created remain good and happy?* All the angels God created did not remain good and happy; many of them sinned and were cast into hell, and these are called devils or bad angels.
2. *What was the devil's name before he fell, and why was he cast out of heaven?* Before he fell, Satan, or the devil, was called Lucifer, or light-bearer, a name which indicates great beauty. He was cast out of heaven because through pride he rebelled against God.
3. *How do the bad angels act toward us?* The bad angels try by every means to lead us into sin. The efforts they make are called the temptations of the devil.
4. *Why does the devil tempt us?* The devil tempts us because he hates goodness, and does not wish us to enjoy the happiness which he himself has lost.
5. *Can we by our own power overcome the temptations of the devil?* We cannot by our own power overcome the temptations of the devil, because the devil is wiser than we are; for, being an angel, he is more intelligent, and he did not lose his intelligence by

falling into sin any more than we do now. Therefore, to overcome his temptations, we need the help of God.

6. *What do we promise in Baptism?* In Baptism, we promise to renounce the devil, with all his works and pomps.

7. *What do we mean by the "pomps" of the devil?* By the pomps of the devil, we mean all worldly pride, vanities, and vain shows by which people are enticed into sin, and all foolish or sinful display of ourselves or of what we possess.

Prayer of Service to God

Prayer of St. Teresa of Avila

God of love,
Help us to remember that
Christ has no body now on earth but ours,
no hands but ours, no feet but ours.
Ours are the eyes to see the needs of the world.
Ours are the hands with which to bless everyone now.
Ours are the feet with which He is
to go about doing good. Amen.

"Visiting Card" of Blessed Mother Teresa of Calcutta

The fruit of silence is prayer;
the fruit of prayer is faith;
the fruit of faith is love;
the fruit of love is service;
the fruit of service is peace.
This is the way to meet Christ.

HEAVEN

T ODAY," Auntie began, "we are going to do some very sensible thinking." The children looked rather alarmed. "Sensible" sounded dull and tiresome. Grown people had to be sensible, they supposed. Would Auntie really expect little lambs to be anything so strange and uncomfortable?

Auntie laughed mischievously. "We're going to be even something more than sensible," said she; "we're going to be positively business-like."

This was awful. Philip dimly wondered whether Auntie would ask him to multiply the daisies Anna held in her lap—there were eight of them—by some hard number. Rose thought of the five dollars and nine cents in her bank, and was ready to give it up at once, if Auntie meant anything like that. Rose had made a private resolve to be very generous because the Good Shepherd was so generous with His little lambs. John simply waited, and Anna, throwing her head back, sank into cozy limpness, as much as to say, "This is too much for me, so I'll take a nap!"

"You don't seem pleased," said Auntie.

"I think," said John, "we don't quite understand."

"But I know you will," said Auntie. "We are going to consider the value of things."

"Anna can't," said Rose hastily. "She counts awfully."

"I don't," Anna contradicted; "I let John count."

"Anna can consider the values I'm going to talk about exactly as well as the rest. We'll have Anna answer my first question."

Anna wriggled uncomfortably. She had no ambition to be questioned.

"Would you give your best doll, Anna, for that bit of wood in the road?" Auntie asked, nodding towards a miserable stick.

Anna looked immensely relieved. The answer was easy. "Of course not," said she. "My best doll is beautiful, and nobody wants that horrid bit of wood."

"Philip," Auntie went on, "would you exchange your toy trucks for a pencil?"

"No, indeed, Auntie." Philip spoke very decidedly. He liked nice pencils, with long sharp points. But pencils were to be despised when toy trucks were in question. Auntie might have known without asking.

"You see, we're not so unfit for business, after all, are we?" laughed Auntie. "Would you rather have an apple, John, instead of your new book about plants?" The book was a wonder and full of pictures in color.

"No, Auntie." John did not hesitate. His love for the book was very real.

Auntie began to look solemn.

"Rose is the only one left. I'm not afraid that she'll be any less business-like than the others. Rose, dear, would you rather have Mother's piano, or a toy violin?"

"Why, Auntie! I'd rather have Mother's piano."

Auntie nodded her head.

"I knew how it would be," said she gravely.

"You wouldn't want us to be silly, would you, Auntie?" Philip asked. "When we know what is good, we choose it."

"Naturally. You are sensible. Remember, I told you that we were going to consider things in a sensible manner."

Smiles fairly flooded the yard. The children were no longer alarmed about Auntie's sensible morning.

"Let's have a few more questions," Auntie encouraged. "We'll agree first, that anyone of you given the choice between something useless and something very nice, would take the thing that was very nice. Now tell me this: If there were two things equally nice, and you could have one for a single moment and the other for a week, which one would you choose?"

"The one for a week," answered Rose, Philip, and John together.

"Yes," said Anna afterward, "I think so, too."

"The whole world thinks so," said Auntie. "It's wonderful how shrewd and clever people are when earthly things are at stake. That is why our Lord once said that worldly people were wiser than the children of light."

"Did He mean us?" Philip asked.

"By the children of light, our Lord meant people who know His Truth, and try to follow Him. We are some of those of whom our Lord spoke."

"It sounds pretty, Auntie," said Rose: "children of light!"

"To be children of light is one of our dearest privileges. Jesus said, at another time, that those who followed Him did not walk in darkness."

"They couldn't," John said slowly, "because Jesus is the Light of the World, and when we walk close to Him, it can't be dark."

"What we need to do," Auntie went on, "is to ask our Lord to give us freely of His light, so we shall not let children of the world be ahead of us in wisdom. We want to be more anxious and clever about the things of God than they are about the affairs of earth. The other day you were playing with soap bubbles, and little Anna cried out, 'They shine like Mommy's pearls!' Yet you all know how a breath will destroy a soap bubble, beautiful as it is, and nobody ever was or ever will be able to grasp a soap bubble and carry it about."

"And Mother wears the pearls," said John thoughtfully, "and they were Grandmother's and Great-grandmother's."

"They are even much older than Father!" said Anna, drawing a deep breath at the thought.

The older children laughed, and Philip, forgetting all his good resolutions, exclaimed, "Of course, silly! Uncle Edward is quite a young man. I heard Mother say so."

"And the pearls are very old," said Auntie, shaking her head at Philip. "But they stay just as lovely as can be. You wouldn't give them away for some soap bubbles, would you, Anna?"

"No, indeed!" declared Anna.

"Well, while there is a very big difference between the value of pearls and soap bubbles, there is more difference than ever could be measured between the things of earth and the things of heaven. Heaps of our joys melt away like soap bubbles almost as soon as we have them. And the best of them can't last forever. Now let's consider very sensibly and in a businesslike fashion which we intend to choose." Auntie spoke very slowly, and after she said "choose," she stopped.

The children sat very still. A mother robin, looking for food for her babies, hopped quite close, the little lambs looked so quiet and harmless.

"Can't we have any fun?" Philip stirred uneasily as he put the question after a long pause.

"Why, you may have all the fun in the world," said Auntie heartily, "as long as it is not sin. I believe fun helps us to be good little lambs. And I am positive the Good Shepherd particularly loves happy hearts. We're not going to choose sadness, when we are specially invited to be happy at our Lord's own Feast. You forget that we are bound to be sensible, not foolish."

"It's sensible to be happy?" suggested Philip.

"It's sensible, and it's a sign of our gratitude to our Good Shepherd."

"The sheep on the hill are very happy," said John. "They have plenty to eat, and soft grass to lie down on, and the sun to keep them warm. And when there is a bad storm, they are put under shelter."

"And Bruce watches them," added Anna. "He is a very good doggie, Auntie."

"He is the best doggie in the world," Auntie declared. "And the sheep are grateful and contented. Now we have souls as well as bodies, and our Good Shepherd is the Lord Jesus. We thank Him for His loving care, and we rejoice that we are His sheep. The best of it is, we are His sheep forever and ever—if we choose."

"In heaven," said Rose.

"In heaven," Auntie repeated. "Listen carefully, little lambs: If you were offered all the beauty, every bit of the wealth, the entire love, and the complete happiness of the whole world, these things would, altogether, be

as worthless as the soap bubble compared with heaven.
Do you know why?"

"Because," Rose eagerly began, "Heaven is beauti-
fuler—no, more beautiful—and—and happier, and—"
she stopped for a word.

"It's perfect, Mother says," said Philip. "We can't even
imagine it, because everything we know about has something imperfect in it."

Rose sighed admiringly. She was sure that when
Philip grew up he would know more than anybody else
in the whole world, except, of course, her father.

"It is lovelier than the most beautiful dream," said
Auntie; "we shall see God in heaven—see Him as He is."

"In this world," said John, "we see Him in the Sacred Host."

"Yes, we see Him hidden under the appearance of
the Host. In heaven, our faith will be rewarded by our
seeing Him face to face, the way the angels see Him.
And there will be no more danger of losing Him."

"We need not choose any more," said John.

"No, we'll be safe forever. There is another reason
why the whole world would not be worth the loss of
heaven: Heaven lasts forever, everything here must end.
Suppose a man could be absolutely certain that he could
possess every joy of earth for a hundred years; the hundred years would end, wouldn't they?"

"They'd be dreadfully long," said Rose. Auntie smiled.

"Say ten-times-a-hundred years, if you like," Auntie
said.

"They'd end anyway," said Philip.

"Everything we can measure or count will end," said
Auntie. "And if the man who had been wonderfully happy for a thousand years had given up his right to heav-

en in order to buy the happiness, at the end of the thousand years, he would be doomed to unending misery. He could never see God, never serve among the angels; instead he would have to leave the things he had thought so valuable in this life, and go to live with Satan in hell. What sort of bargain would you consider the one he made?"

"Awful," said Rose very seriously.

"Nobody lives a thousand years, very few live a hundred. So those who choose pleasures here at the price of sin, instead of the faithful service of God of which we talked yesterday, exchange heaven for a very poor, small matter of a few years in this world. Little lambs, you will be too sensible to act that way. The Good Shepherd has called you because He loves you and wants you. Stay in His fold, where it is easy to hear His voice. Never forget that you have renounced Satan, with all his works and pomps."

"And given ourselves to Jesus Christ forever," John repeated.

"It is your part to serve, God's to reward," said Auntie. "The service is only for a time, and is never too hard. Little lambs, the reward is to live forever with your Good Shepherd, face to face, seeing Him as He is, in heaven."

"And," said Anna, "we are going to be sensible; not like the silly man." She smiled invitingly at John. But John's eyes were looking far away. Anna slipped from Auntie's lap and stole over to take John's hand.

"We're going to heaven, aren't we, Brother John?" she asked brightly.

John started.

"Yes, little sister," he answered. "And Jesus will know us. You know He said, 'I know mine and mine know Me.'"

"That will make heaven so beautiful," said Auntie.

"He knows us now, too," said Anna comfortably. "His own dear little lambs!"

Rose and Philip would have laughed, but Auntie checked them.

"Anna is right," she said. "Jesus knows you, and in Holy Communion He is going to give you a little bit of heaven in this world. You know, heaven is the possession of God; and in Holy Communion Jesus comes to you. Now ask the Good Shepherd to make you so happy when you welcome Him that at least in a faint, dim way, you may have some understanding of what that dear beautiful word means: Heaven!"

Biblical Passages
1. Read John 8:12, John 12:35-36, and Ephesians 5:8-17.
2. Read Matthew 16:24-27.

POEM TO READ Aloud
"How God Will Reward Me" by Sr. Mary Josita, OSF

*My soul came from Your hand, dear Lord, and one day
You will call,*
*To take me to Your Father's house, with saints and
angels all.*
*There I shall see Your Father's face, and be near Mary
too.*
I'll see the angels flying through the sky of azure blue.

*Oh, how I long for that far time, like summer, warm
and sweet.*
*When I shall be with those I love, play at the Savior's
feet.*
*Some day You'll come to call my soul, and I will fly on
high.*
My body will be in the grave, but not my soul—not I.

*I shall be skipping with the saints through heaven's
holy halls,*
*Or making pretty daisy wreaths to hang on golden
walls.*
*And then another day will come when you will call the
roll,*
And my body, too, will rise again to join my happy soul.

*And when the angel calls again, dear God, I'll take Your
hand.*
*And You will lead me safe across to that bright, happy
land.*
For me and all my dear ones, new life will then begin,
*And we will sing, "Rise up, you gates, the King is
entering in."*

Prayers to the Gentle Christ

Eyes of Jesus, look on me.
Lips of Jesus, smile on me.
Ears of Jesus, hear me.
Arms of Jesus, enfold me.
Hands of Jesus, bless me.
Feet of Jesus, guide me.
Voice of Jesus, speak to me.
Heart of Jesus, love me.
Spirit of Jesus, abide in me.
Now and forever. Amen.

Lord Jesus, I give You my hands to do Your work.
I give You my feet to go Your way.
I give You my eyes to see as You see.
I give You my ears to hear as You hear.
I give You my tongue to speak as You speak.
I give You my heart that You may love in me
Your Father and all mankind.
I give You my spirit that it may be
You who prays in me.
I give You my whole self, Lord Jesus, that it may be
You who grows, works, loves, and prays in me.
Amen.

The Happy Day

T OMORROW morning," said Auntie, with such shining eyes that John watched them and wondered what news Auntie had; because John had already found out that grown-up people's eyes only shone like that when something very lovely and very unexpected had happened, "tomorrow morning," Auntie repeated, "your happy day will have arrived."

Three faces beamed. Anna looked troubled. The littlest lamb of all suddenly felt very much left out of things. That "next time" of which she had so often spoken seemed terribly far off. The Good Shepherd was coming to the other three, and not to her! And she did love the Good Shepherd; she knew she did. The big eyes filled with big tears.

"And," said Auntie, putting her arms about Anna, "I have something beautiful to tell you."

"Oh, Auntie, what is it?" cried the three older children. Anna could not speak. She was trying very hard to keep those big tears from falling.

"Anna's mother and I had a long talk with our dear pastor; and what do you think?" Auntie's arms about Anna grew tighter.

"Is—" John stopped and swallowed hard. He was afraid to put the question that came to his mind, because Anna was his sister.

"The Good Shepherd is to come to all His little lambs tomorrow—even to the littlest."

"Me?" almost screamed Anna. The tears overflowed, but just because Anna forgot there were any. "Me? Auntie, really, truly?"

"To you, our dear littlest lamb of all," answered Auntie.

Anna clapped her chubby hands and laughed so loud that a bird answered, thinking she was trying to talk to him in his own language.

"Oh, I'm so glad, I'm so glad. Brother John, aren't you?" The child danced from John to Rose, from Rose to Philip, kissing each one, and finally throwing herself again into Auntie's lap.

"I'm as glad as you are," whispered John in the ear almost hidden by Anna's curls.

"We're all delighted," smiled Auntie, kissing the ear into which John had whispered.

The bird overhead sang as loud as he could. Anna had become very still. Her eyes were closed. Suddenly, she pulled Auntie's head down.

"I've told the Good Shepherd how glad I am," breathed Anna, "and how much I love Him."

Nobody in the whole world was any happier than Auntie and the four children under the elm tree.

"Everything is lovely, isn't it?" asked Rose. "My lamb is well again, too. It hardly limped at all when it ran to meet me before breakfast."

"And Grandfather and Grandmother will be here this afternoon," announced Philip. Philip dearly loved company.

"Grandmother is fetching me a gold cross her grand-mother gave to her when she made her First Com-munion," said Rose.

"I haven't any gold cross," said Anna. "But I don't mind, because I can receive the Good Shepherd."

Auntie remembered a tiny gold cross of her own. Anna loved gifts, especially shiny gold ones; Auntie knew how much the little heart had changed when the lit-tlest lamb of all did not regret that Rose would receive a present while she did not. Remembering the tiny gold cross, Auntie decided it should be a surprise for Anna after First Communion.

"The Good Shepherd is the very best gift God Him-self can give us," said Auntie. "Today we ought to think as much as we can about that Gift. If we think about it, we'll intend never to be ungrateful. When we have accepted the smallest present from a friend, don't we feel it would be simply impossible to be rude to that friend?"

"Yes, indeed!" cried Philip. "I know what you mean, Auntie. Last summer there was a boy at the beach who—" Philip hesitated, "who didn't play the way the other boys wanted. I couldn't like him. But when my birthday came, he sent me a toy truck and I felt so ashamed, I didn't know what to do."

"You were always awfully good to him, Phil," said John, "and you made the other boys treat him fairly, no matter how upset they were."

"Still," said Philip, "it was the gift that made me feel shabby. I'd never have liked him, only for that gift."

"That exactly explains what I mean," said Auntie. "A gift softens our hearts, no matter how hard they may be. Philip did not love the lad at the beach. Yet Philip's heart filled with gratitude when the skates came. If a card or a gift comes from somebody we love very much, we are even happier. Some sweets, a picture book, perhaps some flowers—if a very dear friend gives us any of these, aren't we happy?"

"Yes, indeed," cried the children.

"Besides, the more anyone loves us, the more certain is it that a present from that person will be exactly what we most wished."

"The way Mother finds out long before Christmas what will please us best," said Rose.

"And Mommy gives us the nicest things!" added Anna.

"Mothers don't mind the trouble about finding what little lambs long to have. Fathers and mothers are very busy before Christmas, as we all know, choosing gifts for the children. It is love that makes them so happy and anxious. And love makes the children like Father's and Mother's gifts best of all. Now God loves His little lambs more than the best of fathers and mothers can love them."

Anna closed her eyes tight and tried to imagine how dearly God loved her.

"And God gives us Himself in Holy Communion," Auntie went on.

"Then," said John slowly, "God is the Giver and God is the Gift."

"Yes. God gives us Holy Communion and He is Holy Communion. Now little lambs can't be expected to think of ever so many things at once. You don't know it, but it is true that thinking gets better by practice, like everything else. Being very little and very young, you haven't had time to practice much thinking. The Good Shepherd understands. Perhaps, though, there isn't a single little lamb who can't remember very plainly two things for Holy Communion. The white Sacred Host is Jesus, the Good Shepherd—really and truly Himself. There is thought Number One."

"We could think about that a long time, Auntie," said John.

"The way He stays in the tabernacle," said Rose.

"Waiting for us," added Philip.

"And coming to us!" cried Anna in a burst of delight.

"The other thought I'm sure you will be able to keep in your minds," said Auntie, "is that you should welcome the Good Shepherd with love. He is so glad to come to you! Be glad to receive Him. He is the great, good God. He can do anything. Ask Him to teach you to love Him more and more."

"When you love people," said Rose, "Mother says it is very easy to work for them."

"Love makes everything easy. Love the Good Shepherd, and you will do His Will. Love Him, and you will hate sin because it displeases Him. Would you turn away from the beautiful, tender Shepherd, to be with anything as ugly as sin?"

"No, Auntie," said Rose earnestly.

"Jesus will come into your souls tomorrow. He will make them like heaven, because the joy of heaven is being with God. He is not sending an angel to visit you; He is coming Himself. He will not ask for a gorgeous welcome like people prepare for famous earthly guests. He does not say you must be rich, or clever, or wonderful in any way. Instead He says, 'Little lambs, I am coming because I love you. Love Me back; I don't care how little you are and how little you know. Just love Me, and stay near Me always.'"

"I'll love to stay near Him," said John.

"And we can talk to Him," breathed Rose.

"We never need to be naughty," said Anna solemnly, "because we can look right up at Him if we stay close, can't we, Auntie?"

"Surely, dear."

"We can't see Him with our eyes the way He is," said Philip, "but we know He is there."

"That's faith," said John.

"We do not see Him in the Sacred Host, either," said Auntie. "What you see looks like bread; by faith, we know that only the appearance of bread is there. And under that appearance is Jesus Christ, our Good Shepherd."

"They put lights and flowers on the altar because He is there," said Rose.

"And the lamp burns to show us where He is," said Philip.

"And we genuflect to adore Him," said John. "Auntie, priests can take the Sacred Host and give It to us. And once they were little boys and could only adore Jesus and receive Him like we do now." John could never entirely forget this thought. "They once made their First Communion, too."

"They made very good ones," said Rose decidedly.

Anna sat up straight in the way she had. "Well," she said, "we'll make good ones, too. Don't we love the Good Shepherd?"

"Of course," Auntie answered for the others. "And now, when we have accepted a present, what do we say?"

"Thank you," said Philip promptly.

"It is what we ought to say to Jesus, too. Happy that He came to us, we mustn't forget to thank Him. Love and gratitude ought to fill our hearts at Holy Communion. Gratitude sounds like a very big word, doesn't it? Yet it only means feeling like saying, 'Thank you.'"

"Ought we to stay very still till tomorrow morning?" Rose suddenly asked.

"I can't," cried Anna, slipping to the ground and skipping about. "I'm so glad, I'm so glad!"

"It doesn't matter much," smiled Auntie, "whether you dance like Anna or sit still, if you simply try not to forget that your happy day is almost here."

"We can't forget, Auntie," said John.

"No," said Rose. "I feel like singing."

"So do I," cried Anna. And she started, with her whole heart in her high, childish voice:

> *O, Jesus, Jesus, dearest Lord,*
> *Forgive me if I say*
> *For very love, Thy Sacred Name*
> *A thousand times a day.*

Auntie, Rose, Philip and John joined Anna after the first note. The song went up to the Good Shepherd. It was a song of joy and love and thanksgiving. So it was like the one the angels sing forever in heaven.

Could the Good Shepherd's very little lambs do anything better than join the praises of God's angels, while they waited for their First Communion? The Good Shepherd was coming to them as the Bread of Angels in the Sacred Host.

The song grew louder in the second verse. Perhaps the children did not fully understand the meaning of each single word, but the love and joy and thanksgiving were present in every tone. And Jesus knew their hearts:

I love Thee so, I know not how
My transports to control;
Thy love is like a burning fire
Within my very soul.

Poems to Read Aloud

"A Throne for My King"
by Sr. Mary Josita, OSF

I've built a throne within my heart,
For Jesus is my King.
And when He comes, I'll give to Him
My life and everything.

He made the mighty mountains,
The vales and deep blue seas.
But the hearts of little children
Are greater far than these.

The throne within my little heart
I know will please Him more
Than all the gifts of all the lands
That stretch from shore to shore.

I'll keep my heart all swept and clean,
As throne-rooms ought to be.
Then Jesus will be glad to come,
To make His home with me.

"After Holy Communion"
by Sr. Mary Josita OSF

You have come, my little King.
You're in my heart right now.
To thank You for this visit
I do not know just how.
I welcome You into my heart.
I love Your blessed smile.
I know You left all heaven's joy
To be with me a while.

I've tried each day to make my soul
All beautiful and bright.
I've done the things I knew would be
Most pleasing in Your sight.
Thank You! Thank You, Jesus dear.
I give my heart to You.
Bless me and all the friends I love,
And make them happy, too.

COMMUNION PRAYERS

Prayer of St. Therese of the Child Jesus

My God, I give You my heart.
May it please You to accept it,
so that no creature can take possession of it
but You alone, my good Jesus!

Communion Prayer (attributed to St. Thomas Aquinas)

O Sacrament most Holy,
O Sacrament Divine,
All praise and all thanksgiving,
Be every moment thine.
Amen.

"Little White Guest"

You have come to my heart, dearest Jesus,
I am holding You close to my breast;
I'm telling You over and over,
You are welcome, O Little White Guest.

I love You, I love You, my Jesus,
Oh please do not think I am bold;
Of course, You must know that I love You,
But I'm sure that You like to be told.

I'll whisper, "I love You, my Jesus,"
And ask that we never may part;
I love You, O kind, Loving Jesus
And press You still nearer my heart.

And when I shall meet You in Heaven,
My soul then will lean on Your Breast.
And You will recall our fond meetings,
When You were my little White Guest.

Communion Prayer of St. Pio (for adults)

Stay with me, Lord, for it is necessary to have You present so that I do not forget You. You know how easily I abandon You.

Stay with me, Lord, because I am weak and I need Your strength, that I may not fall so often.

Stay with me, Lord, for You are my life, and without You, I am without fervor.

Stay with me, Lord, for You are my light, and without You, I am in darkness.

Stay with me, Lord, to show me Your will.

Stay with me, Lord, so that I hear Your voice and follow You.

Stay with me, Lord, for I desire to love You very much, and always be in Your company.

Stay with me, Lord, if You wish me to be faithful to You.

Stay with me, Lord, for as poor as my soul is, I wish it to be a place of consolation for You, a nest of love.

Stay with me, Jesus, for it is getting late and the day is coming to a close, and life passes; death, judgment, and eternity approach. It is necessary to renew my strength, so that I will not stop along the way and for that, I need You. It is getting late and death approaches. I fear the darkness, the temptations, the dryness, the cross, the sorrows. Oh how I need You, dear Jesus, in this night of exile!

Stay with me tonight, Jesus, in life with all its dangers, I need You. Let me recognize You as Your disciples did at the breaking of the bread, so that the Eucharistic Communion be the light which disperses the darkness, the force which sustains me, the unique joy of my heart.

Stay with me, Lord, because at the hour of my death, I want to remain united to You, if not by Communion, at least by grace and love.

Stay with me, Jesus. I do not ask for divine consolation, because I do not merit it, but the gift of Your Presence. Oh yes, I ask this of You!

Stay with me, Lord, for it is You alone I look for, Your love, Your grace, Your will, Your heart, Your spirit, because I love You and ask no other reward but to love You more and more. With a firm love, I will love You with all my heart while on earth and continue to love You perfectly during all eternity. Amen.

OTHER RACE FOR HEAVEN PRODUCTS

RACE for Heaven study guides use the saint biographies of Mary Fabyan Windeatt to teach the Catholic faith to all members of your family. Written with your family's various learning levels in mind, these flexible study guides succeed as stand-alone unit studies or supplements to your regular curriculum. Thirty to sixty minutes per day will allow your family to experience:

- ☑ The spirituality and holy habits of the saints
- ☑ Lively family discussions on important faith topics
- ☑ Increased critical thinking and reading comprehension skills
- ☑ Quality read-aloud time with Catholic "living books"
- ☑ Enhanced knowledge of Catholic doctrine and the Bible
- ☑ History and geography incorporated into saintly literature
- ☑ Writing projects based on secular and Catholic historical events and characters

Purchase these guides individually or in the following grade-level packages. (Grades are determined solely on the length of each book in the series.)

Grades 3-4: *St. Thomas Aquinas, The Story of the "Dumb Ox"*; *St. Catherine of Siena, The Girl Who Saw Saints in the Sky*; *Patron Saint of First Communicants, The Story of Blessed Imelda Lambertini*; and *The Miraculous Medal, The Story of Our Lady's Appearances to St. Catherine Labouré*

Grade 5: *St. Rose, First Canonized Saint of the Americas*; *St. Martin de Porres, The Story of the Little Doctor of Lima, Peru*; *King David and His Songs, A Story of the Psalms*; and *Blessed Marie of New France, The Story of the First Missionary Sisters in Canada*

Grade 6: *St. Dominic, Preacher of the Rosary and Founder of the Dominicans; St. Benedict, The Story of the Father of the Western Monks; The Children of Fatima and Our Lady's Message to the World;* and *St. John Masias, Marvelous Dominican Gate-keeper of Lima, Peru*

Grade 7: *The Little Flower, The Story of St. Therese of the Child Jesus; St. Hyacinth, The Story of the Apostle of the North; The Curé of Ars, The Story of St. John Vianney, Patron Saint of Parish Priests;* and *St. Louis de Montfort, The Story of Our Lady's Slave*

Grade 8: *Pauline Jaricot, Foundress of the Living Rosary and the Society for the Propagation of Faith; St. Francis Solano, Wonder-Worker of the New World and Apostle of Argentina and Peru; St. Paul the Apostle, The Story of the Apostle to the Gentiles;* and *St. Margaret Mary, Apostle of the Sacred Heart*

The Windeatt Dictionary: Pre-Vatican II Terms and Catholic Words from Mary Fabyan Windeatt's Saint Biographies explains over 450 Catholic terms and expressions used in this popular saint biography series. Indispensable in expanding knowledge and practice of the Catholic faith, this book provides a ready access for the Catholic vocabulary words used in the RACE for Heaven Windeatt study guides. This dictionary also includes a Catholic book report resource that contains suggestions for forty-five Catholic book reports: fourteen writing projects, ten book report activities, and twenty-one topics for saint biographies.

Graced Encounters with Mary Fabyan Windeatt's Saints: 344 Ways to Imitate the Holy Habits of the Saints is a compilation of the "Growing in Holiness" sections of RACE for Heaven's Catholic study guides for the Windeatt saint biography series and presents 344 examples of saintly behavior, one for nearly every chapter in each of these twenty biographies. Enhance your encounter with the saints by practicing the models of devotion, service, penance, prayer, and virtue offered in this guide.

Communion with the Saints: A Family Preparation Program for First Communion and Beyond in the Spirit of St. Therese imitates St. Therese of the Child Jesus and her family who studied and prayed for sixty-nine days in anticipation of Therese's First Holy Communion. Modeling this preparation, the *Communion with the Saints* program will help any family find renewed fervor in the reception of the Eucharist. This resource includes a chapter-by-chapter study of the following four books:

• *The Little Flower, The Story of Saint Therese of the Child Jesus*—to provide the foundation of God's love for us and to encourage a desire for holiness

• *The Children of Fatima and Our Lady's Message to the World*—to show the sinfulness of our world and the need to avoid sin

• *The Patron Saint of First Communicants, The Story of Blessed Imelda Lambertini*—to inspire devotion to the Sacrament of Holy Communion

• *The King of the Golden City* by Mother Mary Loyola —to illustrate Jesus' Presence as a source of grace necessary to live a holy life

Each of the sixty-nine days of preparation includes read-aloud selections with enrichment activities, meditational readings, catechism lessons, and plenty of practical application to promote a growth in holiness and sanctity. Weekend suggestions include a list of over thirty-five family projects. The use of *My First Communion Journal* is encouraged with this program.

My First Communion Journal in Imitation of Saint Therese of the Child Jesus provides a lasting keepsake of a child's First Holy Communion. Saint Therese of the Child Jesus and her family studied and prayed for sixty-nine days prior to Therese's First Holy Communion. This journal imitates that family model of preparation for the reception of the Most Holy Eucharist. Each daily entry contains a stanza of a poem composed by Saint Therese, a quotation from Saint Faustina Kowalska's diary (*Divine Mercy in My Soul*), or a Scripture quotation. Two weekly themes—a floral theme in imitation of Saint Therese and a battle theme molded from the teachings of Saint Paul—are offered with accompanying weekly passages from Scripture suitable for memorization. This journal may be completed in conjunction with the *Communion with the Saints* program or used separately.

The King of the Golden City Study Edition is a new edition of a book that was originally published in 1921. This treasure of a book was written in response to a student's appeal for instructions along with "little stories" to help her prepare for Holy Communion. To fulfill this request, Mother Loyola of the Bar Convent in York, England, wrote a simple story that illustrates Jesus' desire to share an intimate relationship with each one of His children. This new edition contains some updated language but, quite deliberately, does not contain any pictures. Readers, as they progress through this story, will form a mental image of their King, one as unique and personal as their own relationship with Him. The study sections assist with the allegory, connects to the Bible as well as to the catechism, and explore the art of prayer in the spirit of the three Carmelite Doctors of the Church. Although written over eighty-five years ago for a young child, this book remains a timeless masterpiece of Catholic literature suitable for all ages.

The Outlaws of Ravenhurst Study Edition contains a
classic story of the persecution of Scottish Catholics that
was first written in 1923 and was revised and reprinted in
1950. This 2009 edition of Sr. M. Imelda Wallace's *Outlaws
of Ravenhurst* contains the revised story of 1950 plus chapter-by-chapter aids to assist readers in assimilating the
book's strong Catholic elements into their own lives. The
study section focuses on critical thinking, integration of
biblical teachings, and the study of the virtuous life to
which Christ calls us as mature Catholics. With its empha-
sis on virtues (theological and moral plus the gifts and
fruits of the Holy Spirit), the spiritual and corporal works
of mercy, and the Beatitudes, *Outlaws of Ravenhurst
Study Edition* is a fun and effective catechetical tool for
Catholics preparing for the Sacrament of Confirmation.

***Reading the Saints: Lists of Catholic Books for Chil-
dren Plus Book Collecting Tips for the Home and
School Library*** (formerly entitled *Saintly Resources*) is a
valuable tool for Catholic home educators, classroom teachers, and collectors of Catholic juvenile books. *Reading the
Saints* will help you discover living books from such popular out-of-print Catholic juvenile series as Catholic Treas-
ury, Vision Books, and American Background Books as
well as current series books for young Catholics. Use this
book to find:

- Over 800 Catholic books listed by author, series,
  reading level, century, and geographical location

- More than 275 authors of saint biographies, historical fiction, and poetry written for Catholic juvenile
  readers

- Publishers of Catholic children's books, present and
  past

- Helpful advice for collecting and caring for used books

- Hundreds of age-appropriate, accessible living books to enrich your study of the Catholic Church's rich heritage of saints and notable Catholic historical figures

- Information on how to build and maintain your own library of Catholic juvenile books

- Inspiring quotations about book collecting, reading, and the love of books

Alternative Book Reports for Catholic Students contains forty-five book report ideas to encourage critical thinking for ages seven to fourteen. These ideas are intended to provoke a reflection on those themes and topics that support and encourage Catholic living as well as some that may conflict with our Faith. Many report topics require an examination of our personal faith life and prompt us to take lessons from the saints to strengthen our own faith in God. The suggested activities vary from written exercises to creative art projects and include twenty-one topics specifically designed for saint biographies. Other activities can be used within a group or family.

The Family that Overtook Christ Study Edition: The Story of the Family of St. Bernard of Clairvaux is an excellent read for young adults who are preparing to receive the Sacrament of Confirmation. In this exciting chronicle of the life of twelfth-century knights, we have an entire family of nine saints who lay before us their individual means of achieving intimate union with Christ. Learn with the Fontaines family how to supernaturalize the natural, develop a God-consciousness, and attain sanctity by being yourself. Perfect for high-school read-aloud, this new study edition has over 250 footnotes for increased comprehension and provides discussion/meditation points to promote the art of spiritual conversation. The appendix lists formulas of Catholic doctrine that are essential for confirmands not only to know but also to incorporate into their own spiritual lives.

To Order: Email infoRACEforHeaven.com or place an order from RaceforHeaven.com. Discover, MasterCard, VISA, PayPal, American Express, checks, and money orders are accepted.

www.ingramcontent.com/pod-product-compliance
Lightning Source LLC
LaVergne TN
LVHW011423080426
835512LV00005B/230